ShagMail.com presents...

The Best of
Clean Laffs

~ . ~

www.CleanLaffs.com

Published By ShagMail.com

Copyright 2000 by Penn, LLC & ShagMail.com

Cover Design: PMT, Frankfort, IL

No part of this publication may be reproduced, stored in a retrieval system or transmitted in any form or by any means, electronic, mechanical, photocopying, recording, scanning or otherwise, except as permitted under Sections 107 or 108 of the 1976 United States Copyright Act, without either the prior written permission of the Publisher. Requests to the Publisher for permission should be addressed to the Permissions Department, Penn, LLC, 19001 S. Old LaGrange Rd, Mokena, IL 60448, (708) 478-4500, fax: (708) 478-5470, E-mail: anisa@shagmail.com

All rights reserved under International and Pan-American Copyright Conventions. Published in the United States by Penn, LLC. and ShagMail.com

http://www.shagmail.com

ISBN 1-931258-01-5

First Edition: January 2001

This book is dedicated to Irving the Grasshopper and all of my favorite joke characters. - Clean Laffs Joe

* * * Table of Contents * * *

An Introduction by Clean Laffs Joe...

Hello, and welcome to the introduction. This is usually the part that readers skip over to get to the good stuff in the meaty part of the book, but I would be very disappointed if you did, because I put a lot of effort into writing it. Plus, there's plenty of important information in here that you won't want to miss; like the origins of Clean Laffs, what you can expect to find inside the book, and the population of Paraguay. So please take a minute to read the introduction. It will do a lot for my ego.

This book is the end result of an effort that began nearly a year and a half ago. That's when I came to work for ShagMail.com and started writing Clean Laffs. Shagmail.com is an email newsletter publisher with more than 70 titles read by nearly nine million subscribers around the English-speaking world. And Clean Laffs is responsible for over 250,000 of those readers. That makes it one of the most widely read joke lists on the web.

From where does this incredible reach come, you ask? It's all thanks to the Internet. The Internet is one of civilization's greatest inventions, ranking right up there with the printing press, radio, television and, I'm sure, a few other very important things. Never has so much information been so readily available. Why, using the Internet, one could find out the price of tea in China from an actual Chinese tea farmer with very little effort.

But the greatest feat the Internet has been able to perform is to give a no-talent hack like me the opportunity to publish a book. Fortunately for you, the content of The Best of Clean Laffs does not rely on my wit. I have read thousands upon thousands of jokes from newsgroups, databases, joke diaries and, of course, submissions by one quarter of a million dedicated and sometimes zealous readers. What I've packed into the following pages is the best of the best that the Internet has to offer. Plus, I couldn't resist including a few excerpts from my personal experiences with life, friends, family and the colorful characters in the ShagMail office. Consider it a personal introduction to TZ, Lewis, Marzee, Kristin, Michele and all the rest.

And every day I receive volumes of new material. It's what keeps Clean Laffs in everybody's email boxes five days a week. I wrote earlier that this book is an end result. What I meant is that The Best of Clean Laffs is just the first chapter in a continuing project to spread fun and mayhem to everyone's email box across the Internet. If you're not subscribed to our little publication be sure to visit our corner of the web and sign up for free. In the meanwhile, sit back and take a few minutes to enjoy some giggles, snickers and guffaws you don't have to feel guilty about.

By the way, the population of Paraguay is 5,585,828. You see how useful the Internet is?

Sincerely,

Clean Laffs Joe

Chapter One

In the Office

Dear Yucksters,

Well, it's actually starting to look like an office around here instead of just a bunch of guys hopped up on coffee and cheese danishes, banging out newsletters and trying to find loopholes in the liable laws. You see, we have recently hired a real, live receptionist!

She's a pleasant young lady named Melissa who has finally brought some professionalism to the place. Up until her arrival we just picked up the phone and said, "Yeah?" Now Melissa says something like, "Thank you for calling Shagmail global headquarters. If you're a bill collector or private investigator, TZ is at lunch. How can I direct your call?" It's all very proficient.

The other day poor Melissa made the faux pas of coming in to the office late. Not the thing to do if you're a recent hiree, especially around here. But her big mistake was the story she used.

Coming up with a good excuse for a tardy Monday morning is delicate business. It has to be plausible, but just bizarre enough to warrant showing up three or four hours late.

She called in with some yarn about how her battery was frozen and she couldn't get her car started. Puleeez! Everybody knows that to fix a frozen battery all you have to do is hit it with a hammer a couple of times.

So I'd like to ask my subscribers to share their experiences by writing in with their best Monday morning excuses. I'll forward them to Melissa and reprint some of the best ones right here.

Laugh it up,

Joe

~ • ~

Second Lieutenant Conroy needed to use a pay phone, but did not have change for a dollar. He saw Private Duncan mopping the floors, and asked him, "Soldier, do you have change for a dollar?"

Private Duncan replied, "Sure."

The Lieutenant gave him an icy stare. He snapped, "That's no way to address a superior officer! Now let's try it again. Private, do you have change for a dollar?"

Private Duncan replied, "No, SIR!"

~ • ~

Dear Yucksters,

Thanks to everybody who wrote in with their best Monday morning excuses. I forwarded them all to Melissa who is now convinced that the entire subscription list is insane and out to get her. She tried to quit and we had to give her a raise. As promised, here are a few excerpts from last week's mail bag:

I had to get my dog baptized. - Ed

MY GOLDFISH DIED - Linda

My dog ate my keys and I had to follow him around with a pooper scooper for HOURS! - Lisa in Tampa

The dog hid my consciousness and it took two hours of searching through my blankets to find it. - Brian
[What's with you guys and the pets?]

We used to have a boss who said that if the wife wanted to have a little fun in the morning, that was OK with him, but that was the only reason we could be late! - John & Patricia
[I hope you mean fun as in an invigorating game of Yatzee. This *IS* Clean Laffs you know.]

When a friend first moved to Oregon from Southern California, he called in, saying he was unable to come in to work that day [because] there was ice on his car! - Hillary
[Wouldn't work here in the Midwest. Anything under 12 inches of snow is still driving weather.]

I am stuck in the blood pressure machine down at the Food Giant. - Glenn

Over the weekend I went mountain climbing. While on a tough climb, I fell. No fractured skull; however, I did contract amnesia. I'll be there as soon as I remember the directions. - Wilma

Laugh it up,

Joe

A man called the undertaker one afternoon and sobbed, "This is Mr. Magillicutty. I need you to bury my wife."

"Mr. Magillicutty? Didn't I bury your wife ten years ago?" the undertaker asked.

"I got married again," the man sobbed.

"Oh," replied the undertaker. "Congratulations."

~ • ~

The manager of a large office noticed a new man one day and called him into his office. "What is your name?" was the first thing the manager asked the new guy.

"John," the new guy replied.

The manager scowled, "Look, I don't know what kind of place you worked at before, but I don't call anyone by their first name. It breeds familiarity and that leads to a breakdown in authority. I refer to my employees by their last name only - Smith, Jones, Baker - that's all. I am to be referred to only as Mr. Robertson. Now that we got that straight, what is your last name?"

The new guy sighed and said, "Darling. John Darling."

"Okay, John, the next thing I want to tell you is..."

A young executive was leaving the office late one evening when he saw the CEO standing in front of a shredder with a piece of paper in his hand.

"Listen," said the CEO, "this is a very important document here, and my secretary has gone for the night. Can you make this thing work?"

"Certainly," said the young executive. He turned the machine on, inserted the paper, and pressed the start button.

"Excellent, excellent!" said the CEO as his paper disappeared inside the machine. "I just need one copy."

~ • ~

The interviewer examined the job application then turned to the prospective employee. "I see you have put ASAP down for the date you are available to start, meaning as soon as possible, of course. However, I see you've put AMAP down for required salary. I don't believe I've ever seen that before, what does it mean?"

The applicant replied, "As Much as Possible!"

~ • ~

I got a job once as a short-order cook. I was preparing a chicken on the rotisserie one night, and as I seasoned the bird I was singing Arrivederci, Roma. Just then a late-night partier shuffled in and said, "You've got a nice voice, mister, but do you know your monkey is on fire?"

Dear Yucksters,

It's true that no good deed goes unpunished. Take, for instance, a situation that occurred today with one of our part-timers, Kristin. She's a high school kid, a typical snotty teenager. And what's more, she's a cheerleader. But despite these handicaps she's still a very nice girl, and particularly hard working. Sometimes too hard.

Today she came into the office with the pallor of someone who belongs in an Intensive Care Unit, eyes bloodshot, nose running and coughing up a storm of airborne antigens wherever she walked. Of course, her desk is right next to mine.

She sat at her computer, doggedly doing data entry while her poor little body was regularly racked with fits of violent coughing.

"Kristin," I said, "you look terrible!" I have the kind of charm that appeals to young people. "Why don't you go home and take some drugs, maybe get a little sleep (before you start an epidemic)?"

"Oh, I'm fine," she answered with a wheeze, "I've just got a little cold."

"A little cold, eh? Are you taking anything for it?"

"No. (cough, cough, wheeze...)"

"Why don't you let me give you some vitamins?" I offered. "500 mg of C, and a little Zinc will do wonders for you!"

"Oooo, I don't take vitamins. They taste nasty."

"These aren't chewables, Kristin. You just swallow them." So with a little cajoling, and after taking several myself just to prove to her they're harmless, I managed to get a couple of pills down her throat. The result was almost immediately catastrophic.

The little ingrate began to complain of a headache, a fever and a sore throat - and she blamed it on the vitamins!

"Kristin!" I cried, "Do you think you might have a headache because you've been coughing so hard I can practically see your lungs?"

"No, I felt fine earlier!" She was deeply offended that I should suggest such an outrageous idea.

So she left early with the excuse that I had "poisoned" her with vitamin C. Where's the justice in that?

I have since earned a reputation around the office as the drug pusher. You need a dime bag of vitamin C? Maybe you want to drop a little Zinc? You come to old Joe and he'll set you up. Now if you'll excuse me, I have to drive my Cadillac downtown to meet my B Complex connection.

Laugh it up,

Joe

Dear Yucksters,

We had a fire alarm at the office today and I was able to observe an unusual phenomenon. Nobody got up and left! That ear-splitting alarm just kept on buzzing while everybody sat at their desks, clacking away on their keyboards. After two minutes TZ finally burst out of his office and screamed, "WHAT THE HECK IS WITH THIS RACKET! ARE WE SUPPOSED TO GO OUTSIDE OR SOMETHING?"

"I DON'T KNOW!" I shouted back over the klaxon, "MAYBE IT'S JUST A TEST! I DON'T SMELL ANY SMOKE OR ANYTHING!"

That seemed to satisfy him, because he went back to his office and slammed the door. Marzee and I went over to the window and looked down at the parking lot where a group of about fifty people had already gathered. We were in the middle of discussing the pros and cons of abandoning work to go outside when an honest to goodness fireman, complete with ax and helmet, opened the door and stared at us for a second.

"HI THERE!" I hollered at the top of my voice.

"FOR GOD'S SAKE, WHAT ARE YOU PEOPLE DOING IN HERE?! YOU'VE GOT TO GET OUT RIGHT NOW!"

To tell you the truth, it was a little embarrassing to have to be chased out of a building by a fireman after an alarm had been going off for ten minutes, but in our defense there was actually no fire. Thank goodness. With our bovine attitude toward danger we would have been barbecue for sure.

So after a lengthy lecture by the fire chief, the boss announced that we will be having fire drills. At the blow of a whistle we have to be downstairs in five minutes.

"That won't give me enough time to back up my work," interjected Lewis. "Make it ten."

That's the 21st century work ethic for you.

Laugh it up,

Joe

~ • ~

I was in the VIP lounge last week en route to Seattle, when I noticed Bill Gates sitting on the couch enjoying a cognac. I was meeting a very important client that was also flying to Seattle with me, but she was running a bit late.

Being the fairly forward person that I am, I approached Mr. Gates and introduced myself. I explained that I was conducting some very important business, and how I would really appreciate it if he could throw a quick 'Hello Chris' at me while I was with my client. He agreed.

Ten minutes later when I was conversing with my client, I felt a tap on my shoulder. It was Bill Gates. I turned around and looked up at him.

He said, "Hey Chris, what's happening?"

I replied, "Beat it Gates. I'm in a meeting."

Dear Yucksters,

I told them it would happen, but they never listen to me. Those computer guys think they know everything. So last week the head computer guy, Wes, tells me he's going to add three more mailing lists onto my server. "Won't adding so many more names overload the machine?" I asked.

"Don't worry about it Joe," he assured me. "I know what I'm doing. I'm the computer guy!" (Well, OK. He didn't exactly sound like that.)

So he started mailing the new lists last week. Anyone want to guess what happened? That server ground to a screeching halt. Normally, the server will send about forty thousand emails an hour if it's not operating at one hundred percent. But if it goes over one hundred it drops to about ONE thousand an hour.

Needless to say (but I'll say it anyway), an allowance was quickly made for another server. This one's a brand-new, state-of-the-art job, with 650 MHz, 50 gigs of disk space and a fuel-injected, sixteen valve hemi. This bad boy can send up to sixty thousand emails an hour! Do you think Wes put the Clean Laffs list on the new server? Of course not. I guess I shouldn't have called him a cyber-sissy. No worries, though. I sort of like the old server. It's got character.

Laugh it up,

Joe

"Do you believe in life after death?" the boss asked one of his younger employees."

"Yes sir."

"Well, then, that makes everything just fine," the boss went on, "About an hour after you left early yesterday to go to your grandfather's funeral, he stopped in to see you."

~ • ~

"So tell me, Mrs. Smith," asked the interviewer, "have you any other skills you think may be worth mentioning?"

"Actually, yes," said the applicant modestly. "Last year I had two short stories published in national magazines, and I finished my novel."

"Very impressive," he commented, "but I was thinking of skills you could apply during office hours."

Mrs. Smith explained brightly, "Oh, that was during office hours."

~ • ~

"I went to a job interview the other day, the guy asked if I had any questions. I said yes, just one. If you're in a car traveling at the speed of light and you turn your headlights on, does anything happen? He said he couldn't answer that. I told him sorry, but I couldn't work for him then." - Steven Wright

Dear Yucksters,

Now I know how Noah must have felt on the first day of the flood. We had a storm this afternoon - and I mean a storm! It submerged the entire street in front of our building in about ten minutes. It was truly impressive to watch nature at work.

After three or four cars stalled in the flood, the cops finally showed up with a bulldozer. They towed the dead vehicles out and then began taking cars through the water one at a time by plowing the section and letting the driver follow right behind the bull dozer before the water came sloshing back in. The entire staff was glued to the window watching the spectacle. It was very engrossing.

But even more fun than watching people drown their engines was the opportunity to bait one of our high schoolers (now a graduate, I should add). You see, as runoff turned the basin-like sward on the side of the road into a miniature lake, someone quipped, "Hey, it looks like Shag Lake is filling up!" in reference to the name of our web page.

At that Kristin turned to the rest of us with an incredulous look on her face and said, "It's not really called Shag Lake, is it?" Let me remind you that this is the same Kristin who thought I had poisoned her with vitamin C.

In unspoken agreement everyone in the room began nodding their heads. "Yea," "Yep," "You bet!"

"Why do you think we moved into this office?" asked the office manager.

She stared at us all for a long minute before responding in typical teenage fashion, "Nuh-uh!!!"

Oh, yeah. And there's fish in that lake, too!

Laugh it up,

Joe

~ • ~

A driver, parked in an illegal zone, tucked this note under the windshield wiper of his automobile. "I've circled the block for 20 minutes. I'm late for an appointment and if I don't park here I'll lose my job. Forgive us our trespasses."

When he came back, he found a parking ticket and this note: "I've circled the block for 20 years and if I don't give you a ticket, I'll lose my job. Lead us not into temptation."

~ • ~

"The trouble with unemployment is that the minute you wake up in the morning you're on the job." - Slappy White

~ • ~

Seems that a year ago, some Boeing employees on the airfield decided to steal a life raft from one of the 747s. They were successful in getting it out of the plane and home. When they took it for a float on the river, they were surprised by a Coast Guard helicopter coming toward them. It turned out that the chopper was homing in on the emergency locator that is activated when the raft is inflated. They are no longer employed at Boeing.

Dear Yucksters,

I'd like to share a little anecdote that happened in the office the other day. Young Kristin, the editor of our trivia publication, was having trouble with her computer. So she called Wes, the computer guy, over to her desk.

Wes clicked a couple buttons and solved the problem. As he was walking away Kristin called after him, "So, what was wrong?"

And he replied, "It was an ID ten T error."

A puzzled expression ran riot over Kristin's face. "An ID ten T error?" What's that in case I need to fix it again?"

He gave her a grin. "Haven't you ever seen an ID ten T error before?"

"No."

"Write it down," he said, "and I think you'll figure it out."

So she pulled out a piece of paper and marked down, I-D-one-zero-T, and stared at it for a second while Wes beat a hasty retreat. Needless to say he gave Kristin's desk a wide berth the rest of the day.

Laugh it up,

Joe

Dear Yucksters,

I stopped into TZ's office this afternoon around lunch and watched as he finished off a Slim Fast chocolate shake.

"Trying to drop a few kilos, TZ?" I asked.

"Yeah," he burped, "since my wife got pregnant I haven't had time to exercise, so I figure I'll make up for it by cutting out the cheeseburgers and drinking these instead."

He chucked the empty can into the garbage where it landed with a clunk. I peaked in there and saw it was full of cans.

"Didn't the cleaning service come last night?"

"Sure," he said.

"Then where did all those cans come from?"

He became indignant. "What are you talking about, all those cans? I had a couple for breakfast, one around 10:00 and two or three for lunch."

"Doesn't that sort of defeat the purpose?"

"Of course not," he answered, gently patting his midsection, "although I don't think I get the full benefit when I pour them over ice cream."

Well, dieting isn't for everyone.

Laugh it up,

Joe

On some air bases the Air Force is on one side of the field and civilian aircraft use the other side of the field, with the control tower in the middle.

One day on just such a field the tower received a call from an aircraft asking, "What time is it?" The tower responded, "Who is calling?"

The aircraft replied, "What difference does it make?"

The tower replied, "It makes a lot of difference. If it is an American Airlines Flight, it is 3 o'clock. If it is an Air Force, it is 1500 hours. If it is a Navy aircraft, it is 6 bells. If it is an Army aircraft, the big hand is on the 12 and the little hand is on the 3. If it is a Marine Corps aircraft, it's Thursday afternoon. If it's National Guard, it's still a couple of hours until quitting time."

~ • ~

While working as a volunteer at our local Boy Scout Council office, one of the professional staff -- who was wearing street clothes instead of her usual uniform -- was talking about the NATO phonetic alphabet.

She said that she had learned it some years ago and proceeded to recite it. "Alpha, Bravo, Charlie, Delta..."

But, when she got to the letter "U," she stumbled and asked for help.

I offered a hint: "What *aren't* you wearing today?"

"Underwear?" she replied.

Two men were talking about their jobs. "The company where I work is putting in a computer system and it is going to put a lot of people out of work. Have they started that over where you work?"

"Oh," said his friend, "we've been on computers for more than five years but they can't replace me. Nobody has been able to figure out exactly what I do."

~ • ~

Asked why she was leaving her position, a secretary explained in her letter of resignation:

"Dear Boss, My reason for leaving will soon be apparent - and so will I. Signed: Mary."

~ • ~

Employed by the Human Development center of a corporation in the Midwest, a young woman trains employees in proper dress code and etiquette.

One day as she was stepping onto the elevator, a man casually dressed in jeans and a golf shirt got on with her.

Thinking of her responsibilities, she scolded, "Dressed a little casually today, aren't we?"

The man shrugged, "Yeah, well, that's one benefit of owning the company."

Dear Yucksters,

Poor Joe never gets a break. On the way into work this morning I saw TZ in my rearview mirror trying to pass me. It was about 8:24 a.m. and we both had to be at our desks pretending to be productive by 8:30. That gave us just six minutes (including elevator time), and we were still about three blocks away from the office.

Not being one to pass up an opportunity to have some fun, I swerved in front of TZ's beater when he tried to pull into the left lane. Once again I glanced in the rearview to flash him a friendly smile and let him know I was just kidding, but his face had been transformed into a mask of fury. With flecks of foam on his lips he screamed silent expletives at me through his windshield. I couldn't hear what he was yelling, but I don't think his mother would have approved.

I figured I had better cut out the Ben Hur imitation and let him in before he had a heart attack, so I pulled over and he jerked his rolling oil leak into the left lane. By that time our turn was just ahead so I tried to pull in behind him, but that vindictive little sucker just gave me an evil grin and slowed down. I slowed down even more and he slowed down to match me. To keep from getting the Thunderbird rear-ended I had to speed up and completely missed the turning lane. By the time I went around the block and got back to the intersection it was already 8:35.

So I came strolling in ten minutes late and the office manager gave me plenty to listen to. As I passed TZ's desk he piped up,

"Hmmm...a little late this morning, huh Joe? What happened, run into traffic?"

"Yes, I did." I responded. "By the way, I saw your car in the parking lot. How did both of your front tires manage to go flat?"

Laugh it up,

Joe

~ • ~

When the employees of a restaurant attended a fire safety seminar, they watched a fire official demonstrate the proper way to operate an extinguisher.

"Pull the pin like a hand grenade," he explained, "then press the trigger to release the foam."

Later an employee was selected to extinguish a controlled fire in the parking lot. In her nervousness she forgot to pull the pin.

The instructor hinted, "Like a grenade, remember?"

In a burst of confidence she pulled the pin....and hurled the extinguisher at the blaze.

~ • ~

"I'm afraid I was very much the traditionalist. I went down on one knee and dictated a proposal which my secretary faxed over straight away." - Stephen Fry and Hugh Laurie

Dear Yucksters,

I'm not the kind of person to turn my nose up at a good thing, no matter how unappetizing it may seem at first. Today for instance, Marzee, editor of our daily recipe newsletter, was espousing the benefits of udder cream.

"Is that like the absolute, utmost cream you can use?" I asked.

"No Joe," she said, putting on that smile people usually reserve for vacuum-cleaner salesmen. "It's udder cream....like for cows."

I was still trying to get the hang of the idea. "Cows' udders?"

"Yes."

"Chaff much?" I asked.

"I use it on my hands, Joe." She was starting to lose patience, so I figured I would lessen her embarrassment by asking to try it out. She produced a large white tube designed, appropriately enough, with black cow spots. I read the instructions:

"Wash udder and teat parts thoroughly with clean water and soap before each milking to avoid contamination. Apply to the udder, massaging into the skin."

Well, I had just washed my hands, and I haven't been milked recently, so I squeezed out a generous dollop and massaged it into my skin. And it felt wonderful. It soaked in very quickly with no residue, leaving my skin soft and supple.

"Hey, it doesn't even smell!" I commented, sniffing my fingers. "My hands feel great."

"I told you," said Marzee. She held her hand out for the tube back.

I hesitated. "But it's designed for udders, right....?"

"Forget it, Joe. Give me the tube and nobody gets hurt."

What can I say? I've got sensitive skin.

Laugh it up,

Joe

~ • ~

A street person approached a passerby and said, "Sir, would you give me $10 for a cup of coffee?"

"That's ridiculous! Do you really think anyone in their right mind would pay that much for a cup of coffee?"

"Just a yes or no, buddy," the beggar growled. "I don't need a lecture about how to run my business."

~ • ~

The coffee business is getting ridiculous. There's a new coffee company that delivers overnight. It's called Federal Espresso.

Dear Yucksters,

I decided yesterday that I had to reduce my work-related stress. So I asked people around the office what they do to relieve pressure. I got plenty of advice.

JA, the editor of Quote-A-Day, recommended meditation. But I decided I don't have the patience for that. Additionally I'm not quite sure what you're supposed to do other than sit real still until your legs fall asleep. The Daily Recipe author, Marzee, said that cooking always takes her mind off of things (big surprise). But if I can't make it in a one-quart sauce pan in fifteen minutes then I'm baffled. Finally, TZ suggested that I work out to get rid of all that bad energy.

Now that's a solution that makes sense to me! It sounds manly, but it's ambiguous enough to mean almost anything. I could do 90 minutes on a Nautilus machine or walk around the block and call it a workout.

So last night I dug around in the bottom of my closet and produced a venerable weight set that had served me in college. After I had emptied the closet, moved all the weights into the middle of the floor, repacked the closet and stubbed my toe on a ten-pound plate, I was sweating and cursing liberally. It sort of felt like a workout.

To reward myself I popped out and had a couple cheeseburgers. Of course, after all that food I couldn't sleep a wink last night so I feel even worse today than I did last morning. Maybe I should get an audio tape of tropical rainforest sounds?

Laugh it up,

Joe

Dear Yucksters,

Earlier this week I resolved to start working out again. That I haven't seen the inside of a gym in the last 12 months did not occur to me to be a deterent as I was rife with the enthusiasm that comes with ignorance. So I dug out my old weight set and piled it in the middle of the floor where it would inspire me to begin my new regime of training.

The human mind is an inexhaustible well of resourcefulness, I have discovered, because I never did manage to start that work-out. Let me explain. First I decided to have a light snack so I would have the energy to work out. While I was eating I watched TV and HAD to finish the show I had started.

Then I did dishes (can't leave dirty dishes lying around), and I figured as long as I was just going to be standing around lifting weights I might as well knock out a load of laundry. So I went through my hamper and sorted laundry for washing. I sewed on a button that I noticed had fallen off my favorite shirt, and while I was in the bedroom I turned over my mattress.

Back to the front room for another look at the cold, hard, intim-idating pile of weights, and then off to the bathroom to give that tub the good scrubbing it's been needing.

I have to say that this working out routine has made me more productive than I've ever been. I fully intend to leave the weights sitting right in the middle of the room. I think I can have the entire place repainted by Sunday.

Laugh it up,

Joe

Chapter Two

Modern Living

Dear Yucksters,

You'll excuse me if I make my introduction brief today. This morning I battled traffic that would make Steve McQueen turn his Mustang in for a bus token, and the psychological backlash has abbreviated my attention span.

If you live in an urban area you know what I'm talking about. This was the kind of traffic that zooms from zero to forty miles per hour for 50 feet and then screeches to a stop, only to zoom forward again. Then everybody gets so frustrated that by the time you hit an open patch of road it's kill or be killed just to make up an extra couple of minutes. The way people were whizzing around I thought I was in a scene from Ben Hur instead of on the U.S. Interstate system.

When I finally got to the office I was pale with emotional exhaustion. It took me three cups of coffee before I could even speak coherently. Of course, now I'm sitting at my desk, completely wired, waiting to connect to the server. I've been waiting for the last thirty minutes. Modern life is funny that way. It seems like I'm always hurrying up to wait.

But would you give up the frustration if you also had to give up the Internet, email, your Clean Laffs newsletter, microwave popcorn and everything else we've come to accept as normal parts of our daily lives? Well, maybe not your Clean Laffs newsletter, but microwave popcorn surely you'd give up!

Laugh it up,

Joe

~ • ~

A father and son went fishing one day. After a couple hours out in the boat, the boy suddenly became curious about the world around him. He asked his father, "How does this boat float?"

Father thought for a moment, then replied, "I don't rightly know, son."

The boy returned to his contemplation, then turned back to his father, "How do fish breathe underwater?"

Once again the father replied, "Don't rightly know, son."

A little later the boy asked, "Why is the sky blue?"

Again, the father replied. "Don't rightly know, son."

Worried he was going to annoy his father, he says, "Dad, do you mind my asking you all of these questions?"

"Of course not, son. If you don't ask questions ... you'll never learn anything!"

CAVEMAN TECH SUPPORT

Fire help: Me Groog.

Me Lorto. Help. Fire not work.

Fire help: You have flint and stone?

Ugh.

Fire help: You hit them together?

Ugh.

Fire help: What happen?

Fire not work.

Fire help: (sigh) Make spark?

No spark, no fire, me confused. Fire work yesterday.

Fire help: (SIGH) You change rock?

I change nothing.

Fire help: You sure?

Make one change. Stone hot so me soak in stream to cool off.
Only small change, shouldn't keep Lorto from make fire.

Groog grabs club and goes to Lorto's cave

WHAM *WHAM* *WHAM*

Dear Yucksters,

People say I'm a hypochondriac. I don't think that's true. While I'm cautious about the way I live my life, all of my health concerns are completely legitimate. Like the fact that standing in front of the microwave oven can make you sterile. Stop laughing - it's true!

I also refuse to buy a cellular phone because I'm afraid of getting brain cancer. It's not that your brain will rot if you pick up a cell phone once. But X-ray technicians leave the room when they give you an X-ray, right? Because even minimal exposure to X-rays, ten or fifteen times a day, can be harmful. Same thing with cell phones.

I would also recommend not drinking tap water because of all the chemical additives. Try not to use pencils too often, because the lead can be absorbed right through your skin and cause poisoning. And public lavatories? Not on your life!

So while everyone else is running around shortening their lives by breathing on pay phones, swimming in public pools and sticking money in their mouths (OK, not everybody sticks money in their mouth), I'm going to play it smart and safe. Now if you'll excuse me I have to impregnate my boxer shorts with depleted uranium before I heat up my fish sticks.

Laugh it up,

Joe

A guy is in a public toilet, but soon discovers there is no toilet paper on the roll. He calls into the next booth, "Do you have any tissue paper in there?"

"No," comes the reply.

"Do you have any newspaper?"

"Sorry!"

"Ummm, do you have two fives for a ten?"

~ • ~

"Camping isn't what it used to be. 'Honey, I'm going to go get some firewood, do you have change for a twenty?'" - Nick Arnette

~ • ~

A woman saw a little, gray old man rocking in a chair on his porch and decided to start a friendly conversation.

"I couldn't help noticing how happy you look," she said. "What's your secret for a long happy life?"

"I smoke three packs of cigarettes a day," he said. "I also drink a bottle of whiskey a week, eat fatty foods, and never exercise."

"That's amazing," the woman said. "How old are you?"

"Thirty-six."

Dear Yucksters,

I'm afraid I can't tarry over a long salutation. I have to bounce out to the airport tonight and fetch my Dad. He's coming back from Las Vegas where he spent the last two weeks visiting with my brother and sister-in-law and reacquainting himself with some of his grandchildren.

They called the other day to say "hello" and I heard the report that Dad tried his hand at Blackjack. Supposedly he did well. I can just imagine the frustration of the dealer.

Picture a little old man, perched on a stool and peering at the table over the top of his bifocals while the dealer and six other players wait impatiently for him to make a decision. "Hmmm..." he finally concludes after a long moment of concentration, "I think I'll have one more card."

"Blackjack."

"Amazing!" exclaims Dad. "I'm never this lucky at solitaire!"

I only wish I could have been there to see it. But, no time to speculate. Must run.

Laugh it up,

Joe

~ • ~

If you mixed vodka with orange juice and Milk of Magnesia, would you get a Phillips screwdriver?

A man is sitting in the coach section of a flight from New York to Chicago biting his fingernails and sweating profusely. Noticing his disturbed expression, a flight attendant walks over and says, "Sir, can I get you something from the bar to calm you down?"

The man gives a nod of approval while shaking terribly. She comes back with a drink and he downs it quickly. Ten minutes later, the flight attendant sees the same man shaking and biting his nails. She brings him yet another drink.

A half hour later she returns to see that the man is shaking uncontrollably, and apparently crying. "My goodness," the flight attendant says, "I've never seen someone so afraid to fly."

"I'm not afraid of flying," says the man sobbing loudly, "I'm trying to give up drinking."

~ • ~

A stockbroker received notice from the IRS that he was being audited. He showed up at the appointed time and place with all his financial records, then sat for what seemed like hours as the accountant poured over them.

Finally the IRS agent looked up and commented, "You must have been a tremendous fan of Sir Arthur Conan Doyle."

"Why would you say that?" replied the broker.

"Because you've made more brilliant deductions on your last three returns than Sherlock Holmes made in his entire career."

A motorist had a flat tire in front of an insane asylum. He took the wheel off, but when he stood up he tipped over the hubcap containing the bolts, spilling them all down a sewer drain.

A patient, looking through the fence, suggested that the man take one bolt from the remaining three wheels to hold the fourth wheel in place until he could get to a service station.

The motorist thanked his profusely and said, "I don't know why you are in that place."

The patient said, "I'm here for being crazy, not for being stupid."

~ • ~

Last summer, my husband, Steve, took me camping for the first time. At every opportunity, he passed along outdoor-survival lore.

One day we got lost hiking in the deep woods. Steve tried the usual tactics to determine direction - moss on the trees (there was no moss), direction of the sun (it was an overcast day). Just as I was beginning to panic, he spotted a small cabin off in the distance. Steve pulled out his binoculars, studied the cabin, turned and led us right back to our camp.

"That was terrific," I said. "How did you do it?"

"Simple," he replied. "In this part of the country all the TV satellite dishes point south."

It was mealtime during a flight on a small airline in the Northwest. "Would you like dinner?" the flight attendant asked the man seated in front of me.

"What are my choices?" he asked.

"Yes or no," she replied.

~ • ~

A famed English explorer was invited to Dartmouth to tell of his adventures in the African jungle.

"Can you imagine," he demanded, "people so primitive that they love to eat the embryo of certain birds, and slices from the belly of certain animals?

And grind up grass seed, make it into a paste, burn it over a fire, then smear it with a greasy mess they extract from the mammary fluid of certain other animals?"

When the students looked startled by such barbarism, the lecturer added, "What I've been describing, of course, is a breakfast of bacon, eggs and buttered toast."

~ • ~

I was browsing in a souvenir shop when the man next to me struck up a conversation. Just as he was telling me that his wife was getting carried away with her shopping, a brief power shortage caused the lights to flicker overhead.

"Ah," he sighed, "that must be her checking out now."

Dear Yucksters,

It's funny how technology changes our lives. Today was a perfect example. I was going to spend an hour or two practicing on my bike this afternoon, so I wanted to see what the temperature was outside. If the air temperature is sixty degrees it feels like forty on a motorbike. So you can imagine that the temperature is pretty important.

The dilemma is that Shagmail is on the fourth floor of an office building and the windows are all sealed because of the air conditioning. That means a walk down and up eight flights of stairs just to stick my nose outside for a minute. The alternative is to simply log onto the Internet and in ninety seconds I can know the temperature, humidity, dew point and the exact time of sunset, not to mention tomorrow's forecast. So of course I went online.

The irony is that to find the temperature outside of a window twenty feet away from me, I have to access a signal transmitted from a satellite orbiting 36,000 kilometers above the Earth. That's advancement for you.

Laugh it up,

Joe

~ • ~

"The most exciting phrase to hear in science, the one that heralds new discoveries, is not 'Eureka!' (I've found it!), but 'That's funny...'" -Isaac Asimov

Results of a "theories" contest sponsored by Omni magazine:

GRAND PRIZE WINNER:

When a cat is dropped, it always lands on its feet, and when toast is dropped, it always lands with the buttered side facing down. I propose to strap buttered toast to the back of a cat; the two will hover, spinning inches above the ground. With a giant buttered cat array, a high-speed monorail could easily link New York with Chicago.

RUNNER-UP #1:

If an infinite number of rednecks riding in an infinite number of pickup trucks fire an infinite number of shotgun rounds at an infinite number of highway signs, they will eventually produce all the world's great literary works in Braille.

RUNNER-UP #2:

Why Yawning Is Contagious: You yawn to equalize the pressure on your eardrums. This pressure change outside your eardrums unbalances other people's ear pressures, so they must yawn to even it out.

RUNNER-UP #3:

Communist China is technologically underdeveloped because they have no alphabet and therefore cannot use acronyms to communicate ideas at a faster rate.

RUNNER-UP #4:

The earth may spin faster on its axis due to deforestation. Just as a figure skater's rate of spin increases when the arms are brought in close to the body, the cutting of tall trees may cause our planet to spin dangerously fast.

~ • ~

On a recent flight, an elderly passenger kept peering out the window. Since it was totally dark, all she could see was the blinking wing-tip light. Finally, she rang for the flight attendant.

"I'm sorry to bother you," she said, "but I think you should inform the pilot that his left-turn indicator is on and has been for some time."

~ • ~

Every time the man next door headed toward Robinson's house, Robinson knew he was coming to borrow something. "He won't get away with it this time," muttered Robinson to his wife. "Watch this."

"Er, I wonder if you'd be using your power saw this morning," the neighbor began.

"Gee, I'm awfully sorry," said Robinson with a smug look, "but the fact of the matter is, I'll be using it all day."

"In that case," said the neighbor, "you won't be using your golf clubs. Mind if I borrow them?"

Dear Yucksters,

I've seen a lot of stories about people with lung cancer suing tobacco companies and winning huge settlements. Maybe they deserve it. I enjoy the occasional cigar and I've even been known to smoke cigarettes when in the company of other smokers. But if, heaven forbid, I were to ever get sick I don't think I would sue a tobacco company. I'd probably sue Clint Eastwood.

Clint is more responsible for my smoking habit than any cigarette advertisement. I was about 14 years old when I first saw The Good, The Bad and The Ugly. I thought Blondie was so tough the way he chewed on his cigar that I went out the very next day and went to 15 convenience stores until I found one that would sell me tobacco.

Fortunately, I never really became a die-hard smoker. It made me sick to my stomach when I was a kid. But even today I still can't resist the temptation every now and again. I guess it just goes to prove that kids will believe anything they see on TV. Maybe next time I'll tell you about the first time I saw the show Kung Fu.

Laugh it up,

Joe

        ·‒ ● ‒·

"Smoking is one of the leading causes of statistics." - Fletcher Knebel

A man walked into the ladies department and said to the woman behind the counter, "I'd like to buy a bra for my wife."

"Well, there are three types," replied the clerk, "which one would you like?"

"Only three?" asked the man, "What are they?"

The saleslady replied, "The Catholic type, the Salvation Army type, and the Baptist type. Which one do you need?"

Still confused the man asked, "What is the difference between them?"

"It is quite simple. The Catholic type supports the masses, the Salvation Army type lifts up the fallen, and the Baptist type makes mountains out of mole hills."

~ • ~

One night at an economy motel, I ordered a 6:00 a.m. wake-up call. The next morning, I awoke before 6:00, but the phone did not ring until 6:30. "Good morning," a young man said sheepishly. "This is your wake-up call."

Annoyed, I let the hotel worker have it. "You were supposed to call me at 6:00!" I complained. "What if I had a million-dollar deal to close this morning, and you made me miss out on it?"

"Well, sir," the desk clerk quickly replied, "if you had a million-dollar deal to close, you probably wouldn't be staying in this motel!"

Once upon a time the government had a vast scrap yard in the middle of a desert. Congress said someone may steal from it at night; so they created a night watchman, GS-04 position and hired a person for the job.

Then Congress said, "How does the watchman do his job without instruction?" So they created a planning position and hired two (2) people, one person to write the instructions, GS-12 and one person to do time studies, GS-11. Then Congress said, "How will we know the night watchman is doing the tasks correctly?"

So they created a Q.C. position and hired two (2) people, one GS-9 to do the studies and one GS-11 to write the reports. Then Congress said, "How are these people going to get paid?" So they created the following positions, a time keeper, GS-09, and a payroll officer, GS-11, and hired two (2) people.

Then Congress said, "Who will be accountable for all of these people?" So they created an administrative position and hired three (3) people, an admin. officer GM-13, assistant admin. officer GS-12, and a legal secretary GS-08.

Then Congress said, "We have had this command in operation for one year and we are $280,000 over budget, we must cut back overall cost."

So they laid off the night watchman.

~ • ~

"I don't know what's wrong with my television set. I was getting C-Span and the Home Shopping Network on the same station. I actually bought a congressman." - Bruce Baum

The following items were approved in the 14 volume US Budget, agreed upon by the House and Senate Committees, and approved by the White House:

$240,000 grant for development of a two-headed Stethoscope.

$615,000 for renovation of a skating rink in Plattsburg, NY.

$26,500 grant for improving the packaging of fly paper.

$112,350 for brass polish for Marine Corps band servicing the White House.

$84,425 printing allocation for posters to commemorate Bernard W. Trencher, the first settler of Muskegon Heights, MI.

$1,200,000 special allocation to the Dept. of Agriculture to commence a feasibility study of commercial applications of peach seeds.

$312,500 for a sculpture and memorial tablet of Princess Diana, to be erected in Lake Ozark, MO.

$770,000 grant to the College of the Pacific to study the effects of the 1994 devaluation of the Mexican peso, and its effect on the US ball bearing industry.

$2,075,000 to establish The Skateboard Hall of Fame in Palo Alto, CA.

$425,000 special allocation to the Smithsonian to purchase the baseball hit by Babe Ruth as his 60th home run.

$3,000,000 allocation to the District of Columbia to promote a Miss District of Columbia Pageant in year 2000.

$5,325,000 allocation to the National Institute of Health to study alcohol consumption on college campuses.

$12,600 to replace waffle irons in the Congressional dining room.

~ • ~

Dear Yucksters,

I don't think you'll believe this story. Yesterday I called UPS customer service to find out what happened to a package that was supposed to have been delivered a week ago.

My call was answered by an automated option system that sent me into a queue to wait for an attendant. I waited patiently for thirty-five minutes (this is a very important package) and while I waited I did work, sent emails and surfed the Net. By the time somebody picked up the line and said "Can I help you?" I was so surprised that I had to pause and say in a half-sarcastic, half-serious voice, "You know, I can't remember why I called!"

To my immense surprise the attendant said in a distressingly cheery voice like she was a stone's throw away from taking her own life, "OK, when you remember just give a call back," and promptly hung up. I haven't called back yet because I'm still not sure I can control what's going to come out of my mouth when I eventually get someone on the phone.

Laugh it up,

Joe

Dear Yucksters,

I went out to do a little furniture shopping last night and boy did I find a great sofa! But it wasn't easy. The very first place I went to had a showroom about the size of a small European country. After walking around for thirty minutes I was completely lost. There were walls set up to separate the different styles of furniture: contemporary, classic, living, dining, static, motion, it was all very confusing.

I was just making my way through a maze of over-stuffed chairs and ottomans when I espied a great couch tucked away against a wall. It was big, long, soft, comfy and in a very neutral color, the kind of sofa that would pretty much fit in any room. I guess the salesman smelled a sale in the air because no sooner did I ease my behind onto the cushions than he was there next to me, pricelist in hand.

"An excellent selection, sir," he said. "This is one of our most exclusive and limited pieces. Everyone's buying them."

But, despite the near hypnotic sales pitch, I forced myself not to buy it. I have a habit of making impulse buys (mostly because I hate shopping) so I want to look around before I drop seven C's on the first thing I see.

When I told my good friend Michele about it this morning she was very excited for me. "Now that you have a good piece to start from you can build a whole room around it," she said. "The next thing I would get is a Papasan chair to go in the corner, then a nice, dark wood end table, and one of those big standing lamps. And then some pictures on the wall and then some..."

"Hold on Michele," I interupted. "I believe in Shibui. You know, the idea of less is more? I'm very into functionality of design."

She looked at me with a blank expression until Jethro, our Atlanta native circulation director piped in, "We got a word for that where I come from," he said, "it's called poor."

Well, there you have it.

Laugh it up,

Joe

~ • ~

One night a wife found her husband standing over their newborn baby's crib. Silently she watched him. As he stood looking down at the sleeping infant, she saw on his face a mixture of emotions: disbelief, doubt, delight, amazement, enchantment, skepticism.

Touched by this unusual display and the deep emotions it aroused, with eyes glistening she slipped her arm around her husband.

"A penny for your thoughts," she whispered.

"It's amazing!" he replied. "I just can't see how anybody can make a crib like that for only $49.95."

Two gas company servicemen, a senior training supervisor and a young trainee, were out checking meters in a suburban neighborhood. They parked their truck the end of the alley and worked their way to the other end. At the last house, a woman looking out her kitchen window watched the two men as they checked her gas meter.

Finishing the meter check, the senior supervisor challenged his younger coworker to a foot race down the alley back to the truck to prove that an older guy could outrun a younger one.

As they came running up to the truck, they realized the lady from that last house was huffing and puffing right behind them. They stopped and asked her what was wrong.

Gasping for breath, she replied, "When I see two men from the gas company running as hard as you two were, I figured I'd better run too!"

~ • ~

While rummaging through his attic a man found a shoe-repair ticket that was five years old. Figuring that he had nothing to lose, he went to the shop and presented the ticket to the proprietor, who reluctantly began a search for the unclaimed shoes. After ten minutes, the owner reappeared and handed back the ticket.

"Well," asked the customer, "did you find the shoes?"

"Yes," replied the owner, "they'll be ready Tuesday."

One day, an ape escaped from the Bronx Zoo. They searched for him everywhere in every borough. They announced his disappearance on the radio and television as well as in the newspapers, but no one reported seeing the ape.

At last, the ape was found in the New York Public Library. Officials of the zoo and the animal handlers were summoned to the library. They found the ape sitting at a desk in the reading room with two books spread out in front of him. The ape was reading with great concentration. One book was the Bible; the other was a book written by Darwin.

The zookeepers asked the ape what he was doing.

The ape replied, "I'm trying to figure out whether I am my brother's keeper or my keeper's brother."

~ • ~

A guy had been feeling down for so long that he finally decided to seek the aid of a psychiatrist.

He went there, lay on the couch, spilled his guts, then waited for the profound wisdom of the psychiatrist to make him feel better.

The psychiatrist asked him a few questions, took some notes then sat thinking in silence for a few minutes with a puzzled look on his face.

Suddenly, he looked up with an expression of delight and said, "Um, I think your problem is low self-esteem. It's very common among losers."

Dear Yucksters,

I'm freezing to death over here! The Indian Summer we've been enjoying here in the Chicagoland area is finally over, and as the temperature outside has steadily dropped I've noticed a related phenomenon...the temperature inside my apartment has been steadily dropping, too.

Normally, in a modern, industrialized country like the United States, this would not pose much of a problem. But I'm in a new apartment, and I'm kind of embarrassed to say it, but I can't figure out how to operate the furnace.

In my defense let me point out that the thermostat is one of these programmable, thermal interface ports with a touch-sensitive key pad and a liquid crystal display. Now, I'm not a complete idiot, but the furnace in my mom and dad's house where I grew up had a knob. So I was at a small disadvantage here. Even so, through trial and error, I eventually had it figured out.

I programmed a heating cycle to begin at 4:30 in the afternoon and run until 6:00 in the morning, Monday through Friday, with a temperature gradient of five degrees. And then I pressed "Run Program." ....Nada.

By this time the temperature in the room was about 62 degrees and I was standing there with a jacket and stocking cap on. Dumbfounded, I even went into the closet to see if I could find some instructions on the furnace itself, but all it said was Integral, Continuous Gas Carburizing, Endothermic Heating Unit. No help there.

So I was forced to sleep fully clothed last night while a million cubic meters of natural gas was just waiting to be burned. Even worse, the forecast for tonight is snow. If I can't figure it out by then I'm sleeping in the office. At least you'll get my column early tomorrow.

Laugh it up,

Joe

~ • ~

From a Washington Post Report, in which readers were asked to tell Gen-Xers how much harder they had it in the old days:

In my day, we didn't have no rocks. We had to go down to the creek and wash our clothes by beating them with our heads.

In my day, we didn't have hand-held calculators. We had to do addition on our fingers. To subtract, we had to have some fingers amputated.

In my day, we didn't have water. We had to smash together our own hydrogen and oxygen atoms.

Kids today think the world revolves around them. In my day, the sun revolved around the world, and the world was perched on the back of a giant tortoise.

In my day, we didn't have virtual reality. If a one-eyed razorback barbarian warrior was chasing you with an ax, you just had to hope you could outrun him.

Chapter Three
On The Town

Dear Yucksters,

I had dinner with a lady friend this weekend (yes, it happens occasionally) and it gave me opportunity to reflect on all of the dating etiquette I have picked up over the years.

One of the first rules is never pick up a dinner roll by stabbing it with your butter knife. This is only superseded by the "never do a walrus imitation by sticking breadsticks up your nose" rule. But fortunately that tactic has fallen into such disuse that it has practically become extinct.

Rule number 2 is no matter how nervous you are, NEVER have more than two drinks before dinner. The only thing that's worse than a nervous dinner companion is a nervous drunk dinner companion. Pretty much anything that will lead to your date being driven home by the police should be avoided.

Rule number 3 is never order anything that is flavored primarily with raw or roasted garlic. If you tell your date that you can hardly notice her facial hair in the candlelight you will still have a better chance at getting a kiss at the end of the night than if you order a double portion of garlic bread. As a parenthetical note: this rule does not usually apply to first generation Italian girls.

Now you're probably asking yourself why I spent the evening musing over dating etiquette. It seems I discovered a new rule by accident. Never tell your date that you asked to be seated by the window because you told your friends to swing by and see what a hottie you're going out with. One of these days I'll learn to keep my big yap shut.

Laugh it up,

Joe

~ • ~

A well-dressed gentleman entered an upscale restaurant in the East End of Manhattan, and took a seat at the bar.

The bartender came over and asked, "What can I get you to drink, sir?"

The gentleman responded, "Nothing, thank you. I tried alcohol once, didn't like it, and never tried it again."

The bartender was a bit perplexed, but being a friendly sort, he pulled out a pack of cigarettes and offered the gentleman one.

The gentleman refused, saying, "I tried smoking once, didn't like it, and never did it again. The point is, I wouldn't be in here at all, except that I'm waiting for my son."

The bartender retorted, "Your only child, I presume?"

A out-of-towner in New York at the height of the tourist season decided to revisit an uptown restaurant he'd enjoyed on a previous trip to the city.

Finally catching the eye of an overworked waiter, he said, "You know, it's been over five years since I first came in here."

"I'm sorry, but you'll have to wait your turn, sir," replied the waiter with typical New York charm. "I can only serve one table at a time."

~ • ~

A Polar bear walks into a bar and says to the bartender, "I'll have a gin....................... and tonic."

The Bartender says, "What's with the big pause?"

The bear says, "I don't know. My father had them, too!"

~ • ~

The Dangers of Drinking:

ARKANSAS - It seems one customer couldn't wait to buy some beer. He decided that he'd just throw a cinder block through a liquor store window, grab the booze, and run. So he lifted the block and heaved it over his head at the window.

The cinder block bounced back and hit the would-be thief on the head, knocking him unconscious. It seems the liquor store window was made of Plexiglas. The whole event was caught on videotape.

Dear Yucksters,

I hate to say it, but I don't think I'm a young buck anymore. I'm not certain, because I can't tell if it's me that's changing or if it's just everybody else, but what brought it to my mind was a band I went to see this weekend.

I enjoy live music like most folks, but I certainly wasn't prepared for the spectacle I experienced Saturday night. My first clue should have been the abundance of baggy jeans, black T-shirts and nose piercings I noticed when I entered the bar. But I trusted the young lady who brought me there and decided to get a drink before the show started.

Just as we worked our way back toward the stage the band started to play. Well, play is a strong word for it. They began abusing their instruments with reckless abandon and managed to produce a sound that rattled seven hundred dollars worth of dental work right out of my skull. I tried to back away, but my date hooked my elbow and urged me deeper into the melee of pushing bodies.

It was just then that the lead singer approached the microphone. There was no way, I thought, that kid was going to make himself heard over the cacophony the band was producing, but by cracky he began screaming, and I mean screaming, a string of unintelligible gibberish at the top of his lungs.

And the crowd went wild! I don't know why, because he could have been singing in Swahili for all the elocution he had. But there I was, trying to keep my Harvey Wallbanger from spilling all over my favorite houndstooth jacket, when a mosh pit erupt ed all around me. And yes, I'm young enough to know what a mosh pit is, and old enough to stay out of them. This time I wasn't so lucky. I think the jacket is salvageable, but my Florsheims are a total loss.

So, I think I must resign myself to the fact that I'm not a young man anymore. It's well enough, though. Lord knows what my insurance premiums would go up to if they knew I was moshing?

Laugh it up,

Joe

~ • ~

A patron ordered a Manhattan. When it was served there was a piece of parsley floating in the glass.

"What in the world is this?" asked the man.

The bartender peered into the glass and replied, "That's Central Park."

~ • ~

I was nervous the night my husband and I brought our three young sons to an upscale restaurant for the first time. My husband ordered a bottle of wine with the meal. When the waitress brought it, our children became quiet as she began the ritual uncorking. She poured a small amount for me to taste, and then our 6-year-old piped up, "You can fill it up. Mom usually drinks a lot more than that!"

Dear Yucksters,

Well, Bret Maverick I'm not. Last Saturday morning my friend and I stepped onto The Empress Riverboat Casino with the cool, calculating demeanor of professional gamblers. I was decked out in my best suit and tie and felt supremely confident at I sauntered across to the poker table with the savoir faire of James Bond in Dr. No.

I cocked my eye at the dealer and he gestured toward two vacant chairs, "Please Gentlemen, have a seat."

I slid into my chair and casually flipped a bill onto the felt. "Change of a five, my good man."

"Ahem, it's a ten-dollar-a-hand table, sir."

"Oh," I answered, struggling to keep my poise. "Could you hold on a moment?"

After retrieving my prized fifty dollar bill from my shoe we were ready to continue. The dealer picked it up with his thumb and forefinger and changed it for a depressingly small stack of chips. Then, for the next twenty seconds he stared at me until my partner Mason nudged my elbow.

"You've got to place a bet before he can deal," he hissed.

"Sorry," I said as I slid one of my chips out with all the others. Cards were dealt, and when all was said and done I was looking at two chips instead of one.

"Are we done?" I asked, looking around.

"Yes, sir," said the dealer, "You won."

"Hot diggity," I offered nonchalantly. "Let it ride!"

And so it continued until I had amassed a fortune of nearly two hundred dollars. It was a very heady experience, I can tell you. Mason was doing his thing, quietly in the corner, but I was riding high on the crest of success. Every time I won a hand I would jump up and yell "Ka-Ching!"

But greed was a more dangerous opponent than anyone at the table that day. All it took was a short streak of bad luck and I was all the way back down to my original five dollars.

"Would you like to play another hand, sir?" asked the dealer.

"Uuuh, would you take a third-party, out-of-state check?" I asked.

"Security will be able to answer that for you sir," he said.

As it turns out, the answer was no. But despite the fact that I threw away my fifty-five dollars, I at least got an education out of the experience. And the lesson I learned was - Don't play poker! So the next time I scrape together fifty samoleons it's Blackjack, Baby!

Laugh it up,

Joe

An inveterate card player paused before taking his place at the table, and offered up a fervent prayer to his Maker.

"Dear Lord," he murmured with sincerity, "I know you don't approve of my gambling, but just this once, Lord, PLEASE let me break even. I need the money so badly!"

~ • ~

"I wouldn't mind being the last man on Earth - just to see if all of those girls were telling me the truth." - Ronnie Shakes

~ • ~

A college senior took his new girlfriend to a football game. The young couple found seats in the crowded stadium and were watching the action. A substitute was put into the game, and as he was running onto the field to take his position, the boy said to his girlfriend, "Take a good look at that fellow. I expect him to be our best man next year."

His girlfriend snuggled closer and said to the surprised young man, "That's the strangest way I ever heard of for a fellow to propose to a girl. Regardless of how you said it, I accept!"

~ • ~

The other night, my wife and I were going out for dinner. She put on eyebrow pencil, eye shadow, eyeliner, eyelashes, mascara, toner, blush and lipstick, then turned to me and said, "Does this look natural?"

Bartender: "What'll you have?"

Consumer: "A scotch, please."

The bartender hands him the drink, and says, "That'll be five dollars.

The imbiber says, "What are you talking about? I don't owe you anything for this."

A lawyer, sitting nearby and overhearing the conversation, turns to the bartender and offers, "You know, he's got you there. In the original offer, which constitutes a binding contract upon acceptance, there was no specific stipulation of remuneration."

The bartender was not impressed, but says to the smiling drinker, "Okay, you beat me for a drink. But don't ever let me catch you in here again."

The next day, the winner walks into the bar.

The bartender says, "What the heck are you doing in here? I can't believe you've got the audacity to come back!"

"What are you talking about? I've never been in this place in my life!"

"I bet," says the bartender. "You must have a double then."

"Thank you. Make it a scotch."

Dear Yucksters,

Good Monday morning to everybody. I'm writing this issue early, on Friday afternoon, as I have a big weekend planned. I'm heading downtown to the Bluepoint Oyster Bar for, you guessed it, Bluepoint oysters. I have a lady-friend who says eating raw oysters is like sucking snot out of a clam shell, but I happen to like them.

Then it's off to Oktoberfest to soak up a little German culture along with a lot of German beer. Then on Sunday I promised my old friend Billy I would pop over to his house for a barbecue.

I'll tell you how everything goes tomorrow. But for now I promise to raise a stein and do a polka for you. "Roll out the barrel, we'll have a barrel of fun..." Where did I leave my lederhosen?

Laugh it up,

Joe

~ • ~

A customer in an Italian restaurant was so pleased with his meal that he asked to speak to the chef. The owner proudly led him into the kitchen and introduced him to the chef.

"Your veal parmigiana was superb," the customer said. "I just spent a month in Italy, and yours is better than any I ever had over there."

"Naturally," the chef said. "Over there, they use domestic cheese. Ours is imported."

Dear Yucksters,

As I mentioned the other day, I went downtown this weekend to the Bluepoint Oyster Bar for a small feast of oysters on the half shell. It's been a few years since I've actually eaten oysters and I didn't remember if I even liked them, so I talked a young lady-friend into going with me for moral support. That was an adventure.

Now, oysters are a very popular dish. Once they've been shucked you can steam them or deep fry them, and they make great sauces and stuffings, but of course the most popular way to eat them is raw, right out of the half shell. And this last method is what I had to convince my date to try.

When we were finally ensconced at our table I asked the waitress what kind of drink would be the perfect compliment for a raw sea mollusk. I figured if anybody would know it would be the waitress at a restaurant called the Bluepoint Oyster Bar. Her recommendation was something called a Dirty Vodka Martini.

Before we go any further I have to explain what this is. It's prepared like a regular Martini except you remove the pimento and stuff the olive with blue cheese. This makes the Vodka slightly cloudy, hence the name "Dirty."

We had a pair of these concoctions sitting in front of us when our dozen Bluepoints arrived. They were served on a big platter of ice with tubs of horseradish and a bottle of Tabasco sauce. My date eyed them apprehensively so I took the initiative and scooped one onto my little oyster fork. I gave it a dallop of horseradish and just a splash of Tabasco and popped the sucker into my mouth with satisfaction. Then it was her turn.

She pierced her oyster gingerly with one tine and wrinkled her nose in disgust. But under my disapproving eye she proceeded to douse it in red pepper sauce to disguise the flavor. Unfortunately, on its way to her mouth the dripping mess dropped right into her Martini glass with a plop.

So there she sat, empty fork in hand, while what looked like a tongue garnished with an olive floated around in a glass of murky red liquid in front of her. Now, I'm not going to say I made her drink it, but at six dollars a Martini and two dollars an oyster, you can draw your own conclusions.

Laugh it up,

Joe

~ • ~

"Did you ever see the customers in health-food stores? They are pale skinny people who look half-dead. In a steak house you see robust, ruddy people. They're dying, of course, but they look terrific." - Bill Cosby

~ • ~

At a fancy reception a young man was asked by a widow to guess her age. "You must have some idea," she urged when he hesitated.

"I have several ideas," he admitted with a smile, "the trouble is that I don't know whether to make it ten years younger because of your looks of ten years older because of your intelligence."

Planning a weekend of entertaining guests, I made a list of things I needed to do, including taking food out of the freezer and grocery shopping. As it happened, a friend whom I have been promising to take to lunch asked if we could make it that Friday.

So, hopping into the car, I taped my list to the dashboard and went and picked her up. As she settled into the car her face dropped.

"Thanks a lot!" she sulked.

Then I glanced at my list and saw the first item:

"Take out the Turkey."

~ • ~

A young man called his mother and announced excitedly that he had just met the woman of his dreams. Now what should he do?

His mother had an idea: "Why don't you send her flowers, and on the card invite her to your place for a home-cooked meal?"

He thought this was a great strategy, and arranged a date for a week later. His mother called the day after the big date to see how things had gone.

"The evening was a disaster," he moaned.

"Why, didn't she come over?" asked his mother.

"Oh, she came over, but she refused to cook...."

A man was eating a snack while waiting at a bus stop. Next to him sat a lady with her little dog. The ankle-biter became very excited at the smell of food and began jumping up at the man. The owner didn't seem to be the least concerned.

"Do you mind if I throw him a bit?" said the man to the lady.

"Not at all," she replied. Whereupon the man picked the dog up and threw him over a wall.

~ • ~

A customer wanted to ask his attractive waitress for a date, but couldn't get her attention. When he was able to catch her eye, she quickly looked away. Finally he followed her into the kitchen and blurted out his invitation. To his amazement, she readily consented. He said, "Why have you been avoiding me all this time? You wouldn't even make eye contact."

"Oh," replied the waitress," I thought you wanted more coffee."

~ • ~

A unpolished looking gentleman walks into a fancy French restaurant. The maitre d, wanting to get rid of a potential troublemaker says, "Sir, you can't come in here without a tie." The guy argues, but the maitre d is firm.

So the guy goes out to his car, can't find a tie, but locates a pair of jumper cables in the trunk. He wraps them around his neck and walks back into the restaurant.

The maitre d looks at him and reluctantly says, "OK, you can come in, but don't start anything."

Dear Yucksters,

I'm in trouble now. Last week a friend convinced me to sign up for dance lessons. Generally I try to avoid anything that requires more coordination than brushing my teeth, but this particular friend is much more attractive than your run-of-the-mill drinking buddy. So I was persuaded.

Now I have to figure out a way to overcome my natural clumsiness. One of the worst fears a guy has is making a complete idiot of himself in front of a pretty girl. That ranks even higher than accidentally going to work (or school) without your pants on (don't ask).To appreciate my dilemma you have to consider that I'm the guy who almost strangled himself with a Nordic Trak.

So last night was my first class. Am I really the club-footed buffalo that I made myself out to be? You bet. But on the plus side, every other couple there seemed to have feet that were about as dexterous as crowbars.

Even so, it wasn't a pretty sight. The instructor was an older gentleman who wore a bowling shirt that said "Swing is the Thing" across the back, and the students ranged from gangly teenagers to ambling retirees. And then there was us. We were all shuffling around, bumping into each other, and stepping on toes. At one point my date spun right when I turned left and she kneed me squarely in the groin. It was the dance of the living dead.

At the end of 90 minutes we assessed our progress and found that we had learned to count to four. Next class the teacher is promising that we'll tackle five and six. Only seven weeks to go.

Laugh it up,

Joe

A noted psychiatrist was a guest at a blonde gathering, and his hostess naturally broached the subject in which the doctor was most at ease. "Would you mind telling me, Doctor," she asked, "how you detect a mental deficiency in somebody who appears completely normal?"

"Nothing is easier," he replied. "You ask a simple question which anyone should answer with no trouble. If he hesitates, that puts you on the track."

"What sort of question?"

"Well, you might ask him, 'Captain Cook made three trips around the world and died during one of them. Which one?'

The blonde thought a moment, then said with a nervous laugh, "You wouldn't happen to have another example would you? I must confess I don't know much about history."

~ • ~

A Father, passing through his son's college town one night on a business trip, thought he would pay a surprise visit to the boy.

Arriving at the fraternity house, he knocked on the door. After several minutes of knocking, a sleepy voice drifted down from a second floor window, "Whattya want?"

"Does Jimmy Duncan live here?" asked the father.

"Yeah," replied the voice. "Dump him on the front porch and we'll take care of him in the morning."

A tourist was admiring a tribal necklace at a roadside gift shop. "What is it made of?" she asked.

"Alligator's teeth," the Indian replied.

"I suppose," she said patronizingly, "that alligator's teeth mean as much to you as pearls do to us."

"Oh, no," he objected. "Anybody can open an oyster."

~ • ~

A woman got on a bus holding a baby. The bus driver said: "That's the ugliest baby I've ever seen."

In a huff, the woman slammed her fare into the fare box and took an aisle seat near the rear of the bus.

The man seated next to her sensed that she was agitated and asked her what was wrong.

"The bus driver insulted me," she fumed.

The man sympathized and said, "Why, he's a public servant and shouldn't say things to insult passengers."

"You're right!" the woman said, "I think I'll go back up there and give him a piece of my mind!"

"That's a good idea," the man said, "Here, let me hold your monkey."

Dear Yucksters,

Several folks commented on yesterday's issue, writing, "Say it ain't so, Joe. Are you a smoker?" Well, I used to be a smoker, but I quit. I quit buying them, that is. Now-a-days, if someone goes out of their way to force a cigarette between my lips I'll indulge, but normally I'll only treat myself to an occasional cigar.

I think this is a better way than becoming a cold-turkey non-smoker. Many people who quit altogether become somewhat evangelical about it. At a club, once, a young lady I barely knew actually grabbed a burning cigarette out of my mouth and shook it in my face, "Do you know these things are killing you!?"

Great Scott! You mean all those volumes of information about how smoking causes cancer and emphysema and all sorts of nasty respiratory problems, not to mention the warning printed on the very pack is actually true? Thank you for pointing it out.

I think at this stage in the game everybody who can read is pretty much aware of the health risks involved. That is why I broke smoking as a personal habit. But why deny yourself every single pleasure?

Laugh it up,

Joe

~ • ~

"You know what bugs me? People who smoke cigarettes in restaurants. That's why I always carry a water pistol filled with gasoline." - Paul Provenza

Dear Yucksters,

You'll excuse me if I make a few typing errors. I helped my friend Billy move into his new house yesterday and my hands feel like they are full of sand.

Sometimes people take unfair advantage of friends. When I showed up at Billy's old place all I found was an empty 24-foot truck, Billy, his wife and a two-wheel dolly. The basement and the entire garage were full of funiture, boxes and paraphernalia that had to be loaded, driven across town and unloaded.

Around one in the afternoon, just as I was staggering under the weight of a solid oak armoire and faithful Billy was yelling advice from inside the truck, the other "mover" showed up. Mason appeared in sunglasses and baseball cap with a cigarette hanging from his lips, and without preamble asked for an aspirin. And his productivity diminished from there.

If you've never seen three men who know nothing about moving try to load a truck, then try giving three ten-year-olds a slide rule, a T-square and a roll of sheet metal and ask them to create a working model of the space shuttle. You'll get about the same level of confusion. It was like a twisted Three Stooges episode and I regrettfully found myself in the role of Curly.

The miracle occurred when, at nine o'clock last night, we actually finished the job. I've learned not to underestimate my capacity for self abuse, but please don't ask me to help you move.

Laugh it up,

Joe

Chapter Four

All In The Family

Dear Yucksters,

Sometimes dads say the darndest things. I was over at the Old Man's house the other night when the phone rang. Since he was in the other room I answered it. It was my sister from Pennsylvania. She was calling to say thank you for a birthday card Dad had sent her. We exchanged pleasantries for a few minutes and then I went to tell Dad he had a phone call.

"Who is it?" he asked.

"Your daughter." I answered.

"Which one?"

"The good-looking one," I said, being a smart guy. "Go pick up the phone and find out!"

So he toddles into the living room to pick up the receiver, and I hear his half of the conversation.

"Hello.....Oh, it's you! How are you? .... No, no, I had no idea who it was. Joseph just said it was my daughter, and when I asked which one he said, 'the good-looking one.'"

Laugh it up,

Joe

Two good Catholic boys passed an Episcopalian minister. At the sight of the reversed collar, one of them automatically said, "Hello, Father."

The other boy elbowed him in the ribs. "He's no father, you dummy," said the second youth, "He's married and got three kids!"

~ • ~

A loaded minivan pulled into the only remaining campsite. Four children leaped from the vehicle and began feverishly unloading gear and setting up the tent. The boys rushed to gather firewood, while the girls and their mother set up the camp stove and cooking utensils.

A nearby camper marveled to the youngsters' father, "That, sir, is some display of teamwork."

The father replied, "I have a system; no one goes to the bathroom until the camp is set up."

~ • ~

Coming through the door after school one day, Little Johnny hollers out...

"Okay everyone in the house, please stand advised that I, Little Johnny Elvis Smith, have on this date made a complete fool of myself in sex-education class by repeating stories concerning storks as told to me by certain parties residing in this house!"

Morris asks his son, now aged 10, if he knows about the birds and the bees. "I don't want to know!" the child said, bursting into tears. Confused, the father asked his son what was wrong.

"Oh dad," he sobbed, "at age six I got the 'there's no Santa' speech. At age seven I got the 'there's no Easter bunny' speech. Then at age eight you hit me with the 'there's no tooth fairy' speech! If you're going to tell me now that grown-ups don't really have sex, I've got nothing left to live for!"

~ • ~

If you love something, set it free. If it comes back to you, it is yours... If it doesn't, it was never meant to be.

But, if it just sits in your living room, messes up your stuff, eats your food, takes your money, and doesn't appear to realize that you've set it free..... You either married it or gave birth to it.

~ • ~

Little Johnny wanted to go to the zoo and pestered his parents for days. Finally his mother talked his reluctant father into taking him.

"So how was it?" his mother asked when they returned home.

"Great," Little Johnny replied.

"Did you and your father have a good time?" asked his mother.

"Yeah, Daddy liked it too," exclaimed Little Johnny excitedly, "especially when one of the animals came home at 30 to 1!"

Dear Yucksters,

It seems a lot of folks (especially those who have topped 30) are trying to recapture some of the carefree days of their youths. I wonder why? As I remember it, being a kid was a very tough time.

One of the things that sticks out in my childhood memories was the rivalry that existed between the public grammar school where I went, and St. Christina's Catholic school down the street.

Us public school kids would always get out of class around 2:30 in the afternoon and we would make a point to walk past St. Christina's, where the kids didn't get out until 3:30, and yell, "Catholic school STINKS!" This was especially effective during warm Spring days when you could see sweating little faces peeking longingly through the open windows.

But the Catholic school kids always got their revenge. Invariably during the school year there would be a blizzard, or a teachers' strike or something the school would suspend classes for. But they would always add the days back on at the end of the year, until school lasted until practically the end of June. Nuns don't go on strike, so when the school year ended for the Catholic school in May those little suckers would walk by our school every day and yell, "Public school STINKS!"

Like I said, I never thought being a kid was all that enviable. But just to make sure I wasn't missing out on something by not trying to recapture some of my youth, I tried an experiment. I took the stairs down from our fourth floor office yesterday after work, and as I passed the third floor I noticed that the accounting firm there was still in their offices. Glancing around surreptitiously I stuck my head in the door and yelled, "Friedman, Goldberg and Pullen Accounting Professionals STINKS!"

The janitor chased me down three flights of stairs.

Laugh it up,

Joe

~ • ~

A priest is walking down the street one day when he notices a small boy trying to press a doorbell on a house across the street. However, the doorbell is just out of his reach.

After watching the boy's efforts for some time, the priest moves closer to the boy's position. He steps smartly across the street, walks up behind the little fellow and, placing his hand kindly on the child's shoulder leans over and gives the doorbell a ring.

Crouching down to the child's level, the priest smiles benevolently and asks, "And now what, my little man?"

To which the boy turns and yells, "NOW WE RUN!"

~ • ~

Two kids were trying to figure out what game to play. One said, "Let's play doctor."

"Good idea." said the other. "You operate, and I'll sue."

When asked for her occupation, a woman charged with a traffic violation said she was a schoolteacher. The judge rose from the bench. "Madam, I have waited years for a schoolteacher to appear before this court," he smiled with delight. "Now sit down at that table and write 'I will not pass through a red light' five hundred times."

~ • ~

While working for an organization that delivers lunches to elderly people, I used to take my four-year-old daughter on my afternoon rounds. She was unfailingly intrigued by the various appliances of old age, particularly the canes, walkers and wheelchairs.

One day I found her staring at a pair of false teeth soaking in a glass. As I braced myself for the inevitable barrage of questions, she merely turned and whispered, "The tooth fairy will never believe this!"

~ • ~

Mother gave Billy two quarters. One was for his Sunday School offering. The other was for an ice cream cone on the way home from Sunday School.

Billy was flipping one quarter in the air and catching it on the way down. This happened eight times or so when all of a sudden Billy missed catching it. It rolled down the storm sewer and was gone.

Billy looked skyward and prayed, "Sorry, God."

A teacher asked one of her pupils, "Can you name our nation's capital?"

The reply was, "Washington DC."

When asked what "DC" stood for, the pupil added, "Dot com!"

~ • ~

Nine-year-old Joey was asked by his mother what he had learned in Sunday School. "Well, Mom, our teacher told us how God sent Moses behind enemy lines on a rescue mission to lead the Israelites out of Egypt. When he got to the Red Sea, he had his engineers build a pontoon bridge, and all the people walked across safely. He used his walkie-talkie to radio head-quarters and call in an air strike. They sent in bombers to blow up the bridge and all the Israelites were saved."

"Now, Joey, is that REALLY what your teacher taught you?" his mother asked.

"Well, no Mom, but if I told it the way the teacher did, you'd never believe it!"

~ • ~

A professor was giving a big test one day to his students. He handed out all of the tests and went back to his desk to wait. Once the test was over the students all handed the tests back in. The professor noticed that one of the students had attached a $100 bill to his test with a note saying "A dollar per point." The next class the professor handed the tests back out. This student got back his test and $64 change.

Dear Yucksters,

Writing about the seasons and California yesterday brought to the surface some old but cherished memories about hiking in the magnificent Kings Canyon National Park.

There were several of us making that hike including my sister Nicky and brother-in-law Dean. One exhausted afternoon, after pitching camp next to a stream in a very out-of-the-way corner, we made dinner, complained enthusiastically about our blisters and then prepared for sleep.

With our packs slung securely in a tree we were surprised by the arrival of a small party of black bears in the middle of the night. I say small because by the dying embers of the campfire and the faint starlight all we could make out were occasional flashes of greedy eyes, so they could have numbered anywhere from two to five. But at night in the wilderness it's easy to let your imagination run away.

Drudging up every last scrap of bear-lore we could muster while squatting together inside a tent in the pitch black we decided to yell, bang pans, throw things and generally make a cacophony intimidating enough (hopefully) to scare away even a hungry bear.

So we begin banging our cooking gear, throwing sticks and twigs and yelling like idiots at the top of our lungs. Nothing worked. As panic began to set in my sister, in a fit of desperation, picked up a chunk of firewood so big she had to use two hands to lift it, and threw it like a shotput in what she assumed was the direction of the bears.

I don't like to make generalizations, but the old adage about throwing like a girl was proven conclusively when Nicky's projectile, not quite making it the 50 feet to the bears, connected with Dean's head five feet away with an audible thud.

I guess all turned out for the best, because Dean's screams of agony finally managed to scare the bears away and there was surprsingly little blood. But I don't recommend this particular technique when next you're on the trail.

Laugh it up,

Joe

~ • ~

A police officer in a small town stopped a motorist who was speeding down Main Street.

"But officer," the man began, "I can explain."

"Just be quiet," snapped the officer, "or I'm going to add resisting arrest to the charges. You can cool your heels in jail until the chief gets back."

"But officer, I just wanted to say...."

"I said keep quiet! You're going to jail!"

A few hours later the officer looked in on his prisoner and said, "Lucky for you the chief is at his daughter's wedding. He'll be in a good mood when he gets back."

"Don't count on it," answered the fellow, "I'm the groom."

A little boy forgot his lines during a Sunday School play. His mother, sitting in the front row to prompt him, gestured and formed the words silently with her lips, but it didn't help. Her son's memory was blank.

Finally she leaned forward and whispered the cue, "I am the light of the world."

The child beamed and with great feeling and a loud, clear voice said, "My mommy is the light of the world."

~ • ~

Two little children, a boy and a girl, walked hand-in-hand to a neighbor's house. The little girl stood on her tiptoes and was just able to reach the doorbell. Then, an elderly lady greeted them at the front door.

"Good morning, children," she said. "What can I do for you?"

"We're playing house," the little girl answered. "This is my husband and I'm his wife. Can we come in?"

Thoroughly enchanted by the scene, the elderly lady replied, "By all means, do come in."

Once inside, she offered the children lemonade and cookies, which they graciously accepted. When a second tall glass of lemonade was offered, the little girl politely declined. "No thank you," she said. "We have to go now. My husband just wet his pants."

Little Johnny wasn't getting good marks in school. One day he surprised the teacher with an announcement.

He tapped her on the shoulder and said, "I don't want to scare you, but my daddy says if I don't get better grades.... somebody is going to get a spanking."

~ • ~

The teacher asked her class what each wanted to become when they grew up. A chorus of responses came from all over the room. "A football player," "A doctor," "An astronaut," "The president," "A fireman," "A teacher," "A race car driver."

Everyone that is, except Tommy. So she said to him, "Tommy, what do you want to be when you grow up?"

"Possible," Tommy replied.

"Possible?" asked the teacher.

"Yes," Tommy said. "Mom is always telling me I'm impossible. So when I get to be big, I want to be possible."

~ • ~

"Sally, can you spell 'water' for me?" The teacher asked.

"H I J K L M N O!" answered Sally promptly.

Her teacher look puzzled. "That doesn't spell 'water.'"

"Sure it does," said Sally, "It's all the letters from H to O."

Dear Yucksters,

I read the other day how home-schooled kids swept the three top spots in a recent national spelling bee. This is, of course, no big surprise to old Joe who is a product of the Chicago Public School system.

Learning from your parents is a completely different ballgame from the curriculum they spoon feed you in the public schools. I remember Dad trying to teach me the multiplication tables when I was a young 'un. His technique was to stand over me at the kitchen table while I read columns of numbers over and over out loud.

Mr. Chips he wasn't. Eventually his impatience got the better of him and he gave up, which is probably a good thing because I was getting increasingly rebellious and began to go out of my way not to learn anything. I still can't count any higher than six times eight without using my fingers (the answer is forty-eight, by the way).

While public school wasn't much more fun, at least I knew how to survive. I was an excellent spitball-maker and early on I perfected the trick of napping while pretending to read a book in my lap. A technique I still use to this day.

But anyway, 12-year-old George Thampy of Missouri brought home the bacon by spelling (among others): "ersatz," "annelid," "serendipity," "surfactant," "vesicant," "emmetropia," "quodlibet," "eudaemonic," "ditokous," "propaedeutic" and finally "demarche."

I hate to admit it, but I don't even know what most of those words mean except for "serendipity." I'm fairly certain that's a roller coaster ride at Great America.

Laugh it up,

Joe

~ • ~

Little Joe walked into his dad's study while his dad was working on the computer.

"Dad," said Joe, "Remember when you told me you'd give me twenty dollars if I passed my math test?"

Dad nodded.

"Well, the good news is that I just saved you twenty bucks."

~ • ~

"Don't be so hard on your old man. He's tough and he's sweet. Like me. I'm tough and I'm sweet. Look at my two boys...one I put through college, the other I put through a wall." - Lou (Burt Young) in BACK TO SCHOOL

~ • ~

College is a fountain of knowledge... and students are there to drink.

A professor stood before his class of twenty senior organic biology students, about to hand out the final exam.

"I want to say that it's been a pleasure teaching you this semester. I know you've all worked extremely hard and many of you are off to medical school after summer. So that no one gets their GPA messed up because they might have been celebrating a bit too much this week, anyone who would like to opt out of the final exam today will receive a 'B' for the course."

There was much rejoicing in the class as students got up, walked to the front of the class, and took the professor up on his offer. As the last taker left the room, the professor looked out over the handful of remaining students and asked, "Anyone else? This is your last chance." One final student rose up and opted out of the final.

The professor closed the door and took attendance of those students remaining. "I'm glad to see you believe in yourself," he said. "You all get 'A's."

~ • ~

A young mother, paying a visit to a doctor friend, made no attempt to restrain her five-year-old son, who was ransacking an adjoining room.

But finally, an extra loud clatter of bottles did prompt her to say, "I hope, doctor, you don't mind Johnny being in there."

"No," said the doctor calmly. "He'll quiet down when he finds the narcotics."

A woman was trying hard to get the last of the catsup out of the bottle when the phone rang. She asked her four-year-old daughter to answer it.

"It's the minister, Mommy," the child said to her mother. Then she said into the receiver, "Mommy can't come to the phone right now. She's hitting the bottle."

~ • ~

A young mother skeptically examined a new educational toy.

"Isn't this rather complicated for a small boy?" she asked the salesclerk.

"It's designed to adjust your toddler to live in today's world," the shop assistant replied. "Any way he tries to put it together is wrong."

~ • ~

"Vernon, where's your homework?" Miss Martin said sternly to the little boy.

"My dog ate it," was his solemn response.

"Vernon, I've been a teacher for eighteen years. Do you really expect me to believe that story?"

"It's true, Miss Martin, I swear," insisted the boy. "I had to force him, but he ate it!"

Ending his sermon, a preacher announced that he would preach on Noah and the Ark on the following Sunday, and gave the scriptural reference for the congregation to read ahead of time.

A couple of boys noticed something interesting about the placement of the story in the Bible. They slipped into the church and glued two pages of the pulpit Bible together.

The next Sunday, the preacher got up to read his text. "Noah took unto himself a wife," he began, "and she was" - he turned the page to continue - "three hundred cubits long, fifty wide and thirty high."

~ • ~

I have changed my system for labeling homemade freezer meals. I used to carefully note in large clear letters, "Meatloaf" or "Pot Roast" or "Steak and Vegetables" or "Chicken and Dumplings" or "Beef Pot Pie."

However, I used to get frustrated when I asked my husband what he wanted for dinner because he never asked for any of those things. So, I decided to stock the freezer with what he really likes.

If you look in my freezer now you'll see a whole new set of labels. You'll find dinners with neat, legible tags that say: "Whatever," "Anything," "I Don't Know," "I Don't Care," "Something Good," or "Food." My frustration is now reduced because no matter what my husband replies when I ask him what he wants for dinner, I know that it is there waiting.

A father brought his son into the doctor because the boy had a matchbox car shoved up his nose. All the while the doctor was trying to remove the car, the father kept saying, "I just don't know how he did it!"

Finally the doctor managed to remove the little car, and the father and son left.

A few hours later, the father came back with the matchbox shoved up HIS nose. He said, "*Now* I know how he did it!"

~ • ~

I have five siblings - three sisters and two brothers. One night I was chatting with my Mom about how she had changed as a mother from the first child to the last. She told me she had mellowed a lot over the years:

"When your oldest sister coughed or sneezed, I called the ambulance. When your youngest brother swallowed a dime, I just told him it was coming out of his allowance."

~ • ~

A little girl was asked what she wanted most for her birthday and she declared: "A baby brother."

"Daddy and I would like to give you a baby brother," said her mom, "but there isn't time before your birthday."

"Why don't you do like they do down at Daddy's factory when they want something in a hurry? Put more men on the job."

Adam and Eve had an ideal marriage. He didn't have to hear about all the men she could have married, and she didn't have to hear about the way his mother cooked.

~ • ~

One day our physics professor was discussing a particularly complicated concept. A pre-med student rudely interrupted to ask, "Why do we have to learn this stuff?"

"To save lives." the professor responded quickly and continued the lecture.

A few minutes later, the same student spoke up again. "So, how does physics save lives?" he persisted.

"It keeps the ignoramuses out of medical school," replied the professor.

~ • ~

On the weekend of the biggest motorcycle gathering of the year, I was bartending at a club nearby. When the roaring machines pulled up outside, our patrons' eyes swung toward the door and conversation turned into uneasy whispering.

A group of tough-looking bikers walked up to the bar, and one of them asked me where the phone was. I pointed it out, and the silence in the room let everybody overhear what the biker said into the receiver. "Hi, Mom. Just want to let you know I'll be home late tonight."

The pastor was talking to a group of young children about being good and going to heaven. At the end of his talk, he asked, "Where do you want to go?"

"Heaven!" they all piped up.

"And what do you have to do to get there?"

"Be dead!"

~ • ~

A ten-year-old, under the tutelage of her grandmother, was becoming quite knowledgeable about the Bible. Then one day she floored her grandmother by asking, "Which virgin was the mother of Jesus? The Virgin Mary or the King James Virgin?"

~ • ~

Martin had just received his brand new driver's license. The family troops out to the driveway, and climbs in the car, where he is going to take them for a ride for the first time. Dad immediately heads for the back seat, directly behind the newly minted driver.

"I'll bet you're back there to get a change of scenery after all those months of sitting in the front passenger seat teaching me how to drive," says the beaming boy to his father.

"Nope," comes Dad's reply, "I'm going to sit here and kick the back of your seat while you drive, just like you've been doing to me for the past sixteen years."

Dear Yucksters,

When I read today's first joke it reminded me of one of my favorite stories to tell at parties. And, like most good stories, it wasn't all that funny when it happened.

My Junior year in high school I went on a hiking trip to Kings Canyon National Park, California, with my brother Michael, his wife Beth, my sister Nicolette and her husband Dean (yes, the very same hiking trip as the infamous bear attack).

We had been hiking for three days and of all the magnificence California has to offer I had become most familiar with the tops of my boots, as all we had done was hike. But finally, we made camp by a stream with the intent of relaxing for an entire day.

We were going to do a little fishing, a little exploring, and just soak up nature's beauty. We were on a short day hike that very morning when a small avalanche occurred during which I managed to break my foot. I'm not going to mention that I actually started the avalanche as it is inconsequential to the story.

So, I spent the night in the tent with my foot elevated while Michael made an heroic hike back down the trail all by himself to try and find a ranger station (this was when the bears attacked). Fortunately he was successful, because the next afternoon a helicopter arrived and took Michael and me back to the trailhead where he drove me to the nearest hospital.

So let me set the stage: I'm lying on a gurney in the hallway waiting for attention, and Michael, who had been on the trail for four days and smelled like it, was standing next to me. A nurse came up with a clipboard and began asking questions. "What's

your name, where do you live, what's your astrological sign..."
After I told her my life story she turned to Michael, standing
there in his jeans, hiking boots and four-day-old beard, and with
complete sincerity asked, "and are you the doctor?"

I gave her one incredulous look and hopped off the bed. I was
half-way to the receptionist's desk, broken foot and all, by the
time they managed to stop me. I did eventually see a doctor
(complete with white coat and all), but to this day I have an
unnatural fear of California hospitals.

Laugh it up,

Joe

~ • ~

During my surgical residency I was called out of a sound sleep
to the emergency room. Unshaven and with tousled hair, I
showed up with an equally unpresentable medical student. In
the ER we encountered the on-call medical resident and his
student, both neatly attired in clean white lab coats.

The resident said to his student, "You can always tell the sur-
geons by their absolute disregard for appearance."

Two evenings later, I was at a banquet when called to the ER
for yet another emergency.

I was stitching away - wearing a tuxedo - when I encountered
that same medical resident. He looked at me, then said to his
student, "Sure is sensitive to criticism, isn't he?"

A doctor had just delivered twins...a boy and a girl.

The head nurse brought them out for their father to see. He could hardly believe his good fortune. The girl baby had a pink blanket wrapped around her and the boy baby was enclosed in a blue blanket.

He took one step forward just so he could touch the babies and believe they had finally arrived. As he started to touch them the nurse took a step backwards and said, "You can't touch those babies. You aren't sterile!"

With out missing a beat, he said proudly "You're telling ME I'm not sterile!"

~ • ~

"My wife suggested a book for me to read to enhance our relationship. It's titled: 'Women are from Venus, Men are Wrong.'"
- Unknown

~ • ~

One summer evening during a violent thunderstorm a mother was tucking her small boy into bed. She was about to turn off the light when he asked with a tremor in his voice, "Mommy, will you sleep with me tonight?"

The mother smiled. "I can't dear," she said. "I have to sleep in Daddy's room."

The little boy replied with a shaking voice, "The big sissy."

A father is in church with three of his young children, including his five-year-old daughter.

As was customary, he sat in the very front row so that the children could properly witness the service.

During this particular service, the minister was performing the baptism of a tiny infant. The five-year-old was taken by the whole procedure of pouring water over the infant's head.

With a quizzical look on her face, the little girl turned to her father and whispered, "Daddy, why is he brainwashing that baby?"

~ • ~

A man needed to call home, but the only pay phone he could find was already in use. So, he stood to the side and waited for the man to finish talking, thinking it would only be a couple of minutes.

Five minutes went by, and still the man was on the phone. He was just standing there, not saying a word. Ten minutes later, he was still not talking.

Finally, the first man couldn't take it any longer. He tapped the guy on the shoulder and asked if he could use the phone. "I really won't be long," he said, "but I really need to make an important call."

"Hold your horses," responded the man using the pay phone, covering the receiver. "I'm talking to my wife."

Dear Yucksters,

My Dad is from the "old country," and while he has become fairly Americanized over the last forty years, he still networks with folks he knows from back home. I went with him this weekend to visit some of his friends and had my first experience with European coffee.

The coffee most folks drink here in the states is usually finely ground for a delicately bitter, but pleasant drink. That's not the way the Europeans do it.

First off, they don't filter the coffee. The beans are ground into a powder and mixed right in with the water, sort of like instant cocoa. Then it's brought to a boil so the water can completely soak up the flavor of the beans.

I watched all this with some trepidation which was confirmed when the charming woman who prepared the brew poured me a cup. I guess 'pour' is an acceptable word to use, but a more accurate one would be ooze, because the stuff came out like steaming motor oil.

If this concoction had been any thicker I would have needed a spoon. It was like drinking a hot, black milkshake. There was no evidence of cream on the table and I was hesitant to ask because everyone else slurped away at theirs with evident pleasure.

So I tilted the cup back and in a couple of seconds the scalding, black liquid burned a trail over my tongue. The consistency was such that it stuck to the roof of my mouth in a most embarrassing manner. If you've ever given a dog a spoonful of peanut butter you can imagine my predicament.

But the worst part of this experience came shortly after, as the concentrated dose of caffeine began to course through my blood. In the space of ten minutes my heart rate shot up to about 90 beats per minutes and I discovered I couldn't blink any more. I would have asked to see a doctor, but everyone else at the table showed no ill effects whatsoever, so I tried to sit still and chewed through all ten of my fingernails. I think I should be able to get to sleep around Wednesday.

Laugh it up,

Joe

~ • ~

The teacher asked little Johnny if he knows his numbers.

"Yes," he said. "I do. My father taught me."

"Good. What comes after three."

"Four," answers the boy.

"What comes after six?"

"Seven."

"Very good," says the teacher. "Your dad did a good job. What comes after ten?"

"A jack," says little Johnny.

Chapter Five

Say What?

"There's a statistical theory that if you gave a million monkeys typewriters and set them to work, they'd eventually come up with the complete works of Shakespeare. Thanks to the Internet, we now know this isn't true." - Ian Hart

~ • ~

Dear Yucksters,

I love using quotes, they make me seem smarter and funnier than I actually am. And if I can improve my image by exploiting others, who am I to stand on scruples? But for the sake of this book (and international copyright laws) I have tried to give sources for the material in this chapter as honestly and accurately as I can. However, like much of the material in this book, I have garnered the majority of these quotes from Internet sources, so I can only be as accurate as the obsessive-compulsive insomniacs who sat around typing quotes onto the Internet in the first place.

I have tried to be as eclectic as possible in my selection. The only prejudice you may observe is a favoritism toward my favorite author, Unknown.

Laugh it up,

Joe

A member of the Senate, known for his hot temper and acid tongue, explodes one day in mid-session and shouts, "Half of this Senate is made up of cowards and corrupt politicians!"

All the other Senators plead to the angry member that he withdraw his statement, or be removed from the remainder of the session. After a long pause, the angry member accepted.

"Ok," he said, "I withdraw what I said. Half of this Senate is NOT made up of cowards and corrupt politicians!"

~ • ~

"Hanging is too good for a man who makes puns; he should be drawn and quoted." - Fred Allen

~ • ~

A noted professor was asked to give a talk on "Sex". When he was introduced he stood up and said, "Ladies and gentlemen it gives me great pleasure........."

... and then sat down promptly.

~ • ~

A man spoke frantically into the phone, "My wife is pregnant and her contractions are only two minutes apart!"

"Is this her first child?" the doctor asked.

"No, you idiot!" the man shouted, "This is her husband!"

Jones was having trouble with operator assistance. "Ottinwell," he said, "I need the number for George Ottinwell."

Predictably, the operator said, "Would you spell that last name for me, please?"

Jones sighed and began, "O as in Oscar, T as in Thomas, T as in Thomas again, I as in Ivan, W as in Wallace..."

Whereupon the operator interrupted, "W as in what?"

~ • ~

"I haven't committed a crime. What I did was fail to comply with the law." - David Dinkins, New York City Mayor, answering accusations that he failed to pay his taxes.

~ • ~

"China is a big country, inhabited by many Chinese." - Former French President Charles De Gaulle

~ • ~

"We are not without accomplishment. We have managed to distribute poverty equally." - Nguyen Co Thatch, Vietnamese foreign minister

~ • ~

"The scientific theory I like best is that the rings of Saturn are composed entirely of lost airline luggage." - Mark Russell

Statistics show that at the age of seventy, there are five women to every man. Isn't that an ironic time for a guy to get those odds?

~ • ~

"They say such nice things about people at their funerals that it makes me sad to realize that I'm going to miss mine by just a few days." - Garrison Keillor

~ • ~

I had a linguistics professor who said that it's man's ability to use language that makes him the dominant species on the planet. That may be, but I think there's one other important thing that separates us from animals. We aren't afraid of vacuum cleaners.

~ • ~

"On cable TV they have a weather channel - twenty-four hours of weather. We had something like that where I grew up. We called it a window." - Dan Spencer

~ • ~

"Anybody abuse rental cars? If I'm really bored I'll take one to Earl Scheib and have it painted for $29.95. This really messes up their paperwork. The thing that bothers me the most is when you have to return one with a full tank of gas. That used to make me mad. You know what I do now? I just top it off with a garden hose." - Wil Shriner

"I've taken up smoking. My doctor says I'm not getting enough tar in my diet." - Steve Martin

~ • ~

"Recently I performed at an animal rights barbecue." - Adam Christing

~ • ~

"I've been on so many blind dates, I should get a free dog." - Wendy Liebman

~ • ~

"I'm not offended by all the dumb blonde jokes because I know I'm not dumb...and I also know I'm not blonde." - Dolly Parton

~ • ~

A teacher was telling her class about plant names that have the word "dog" in them: dogrose, dogwood, dog violet. She asked the class if they could name another flower with the prefix "dog."

Steven raised his hand and said, "Sure, Miss Jones, how about a 'collie' flower!"

~ • ~

"Catholic Church services are physically demanding. Standing, sitting, kneeling. Standing, sitting, kneeling... Next week I think I'll try the low-impact mass." - Scott Wood

Dear Yucksters,

There are days, and then there are days. Today was a day. And boy what a day! I haven't had a day like today in many a day. But the thing about days is that there is always tomorrow. But as the saying goes, "Tomorrow is another day," so I guess I'm right back where I started.

Laugh it up,

Joe

~ • ~

Knowing that the minister was very fond of cherry brandy, one of the church elders offered to present him with a bottle on one consideration - that the pastor acknowledge receipt of the gift in the church paper.

"Gladly," responded the good man.

When the church magazine came out a few days later, the elder turned at once to the "appreciation" column. There he read: "The minister extends his thanks to Elder Brown for his gift of fruit and for the spirit in which it was given."

~ • ~

"My mother is Jewish, my father is Catholic. I was brought up Catholic, but with a Jewish mind. When I go to confession, I always bring a lawyer with me. 'Bless me, Father, for I have sinned...I think you know Mr. Cohen?'" - Bill Maher

A man goes into a bar very thirsty. He sits down waiting for the bartender to see him. The man next to him calls for the bartender saying, "I'll have another waterloo."

The bartender gives him a tall, ice-cold drink, then asks the newcomer what he would like to drink. Wanting to try this new drink he says, "I'll have a waterloo too."

The bartender gives him a tall, ice-cold drink. He takes a big drink and says "HEY! This isn't any good. It tastes just like water!"

The man next to him looks at the bartender and says, "Well, it IS water...right Lou?"

~ • ~

"Last Spring my son and I planted tomatoes in our backyard. A few months later he was amazed they actually grew. He said we must have a 'Gardening Angel.'" - Robert G. Lee

~ • ~

"In Paris they simply stared when I spoke to them in French; I never did succeed in making those idiots understand their language." - Mark Twain

~ • ~

"After twelve years of therapy my psychiatrist said something that brought tears to my eyes. He said, 'No hablo Ingles.'"
- Ronnie Shakes

"I like to fill my tub up with water, then turn the shower on and act like I'm in a submarine that's been hit." - Steven Wright

~ • ~

Two elderly couples were enjoying friendly conversation when one of the men asked the other, "Fred, how was the memory clinic you went to last month?"

"Outstanding," Fred replied. "They taught us all the latest psychological techniques: visualization, association. It was great."

"Wow! What was the name of the clinic?"

Fred went blank. He thought and thought, but couldn't remember. Then a smile broke across his face and he asked, "What do you call that flower with the long stem and thorns?"

"You mean a rose?"

"Yes, that's it!" He turned to his wife, "Rose, what was the name of that memory clinic?"

~ • ~

"This calls for a particularly subtle blend of psychology and extreme violence." - Vyvyan, The Young Ones

~ • ~

"Veni, vidi, Visa. We came, we saw, we went shopping." - Jan Barrett

"When I was a baby, I kept a diary. Recently, I was rereading it. It said, 'Day 1 - Still tired from the move. Day 2 - Everybody talks to me like I'm an idiot.'" - Steven Wright

~ • ~

It was a cold winter day. An old man walked out onto a frozen lake, cut a hole in the ice and dropped in his fishing line. He was there for almost an hour, without even a nibble, when a young boy walked out onto the ice and cut a hole in the ice not far from him. The young boy dropped his fishing line and minutes later he hooked a Largemouth Bass.

The old man couldn't believe his eyes but chalked it up to plain luck. But, shortly thereafter, the young boy pulled in another large catch.

The young boy kept catching fish after fish. Finally, the old man couldn't take it any longer. "Son, I've been here for over an hour without even a nibble. You've been here only a few minutes and have caught a half dozen fish! How do you do it?"

The boy responded, "Roo raf roo reep ra rums rrarm."

"What was that?" the old man asked.

Again the boy responded, "Roo raf roo reep ra rums rarrm."

"Look, I can't understand a word you're saying."

The boy spit the bait into his hand and said, "You have to keep the worms warm!"

Dear Yucksters,

Wow, was it a gorgeous weekend. My only regret is that I did not take the opportunity to barbeque. Today (Sunday) would have been a perfect day for it. Barbequing, to me, is an important part of who I am. It helps to define me as a man. Cooking meat over flame, burning the heck out of my fingers while trying to turn the food, it's all very primal.

I have a certain ritual that I do whenever I barbeque. I'm much too impatient to wait for the coals to go from black to white, so as soon as the initial fire dies down I start to blow on the coals. This acts as a sort of bellows to make the coals get hotter faster. The result is a quicker meal, and a mild case of hyperventilation. But the best things in life always come with a little pain, don't they?

No, I'm asking seriously. Don't they? Because if they don't, then I'm doing a lot of things wrong!

Laugh it up,

Joe

~ • ~

As an inspirational measure, the Boss had placed a sign in the restroom directly above the sink. It had a single word on it -- "Think!"

The next day he went to the restroom, he looked at the sign and right below it, above the soap dispenser, someone had carefully lettered another sign which read -- "Thoap!"

"He was the world's only armless sculptor. He put the chisel in his mouth and his wife hit him on the back of the head with a mallet." - Fred Allen

~ • ~

"Writing is easy. All you have to do is stare at a blank sheet of paper until drops of blood form on your forehead." - Gene Fowler

~ • ~

[I don't know where this item came from, but it's supposed to be an excerpt from a BBC radio broadcast. If it's real it's hilarious. And even if it's not it's still pretty funny.]

Presenter (to paleontologist): "So what would happen if you mated the woolly mammoth with, say, an elephant?"

Expert: "Well, in the same way that a horse and a donkey produce a mule, we'd get a sort of half-mammoth."

Presenter: "So it'd be like some sort of hairy gorilla?"

Expert: "Er, well yes, but elephant-shaped, and with tusks."

~ • ~

"A new study claims that mouth-to-mouth resuscitation is not necessary during CPR and it's better to skip right to chest compression. However, the study says that you're still required to snuggle for a half hour afterwards." - Conan O'Brien

COMMENTARY FROM THE WIDE WORLD OF SPORTS:

"Nick Faldo has shown himself to be a worthy world number one by finishing second here today." - Golf commentator.

~ • ~

"And the line-up for the final of the Women's 400 meters hurdles includes three Russians, two East Germans, a Pole, a Swede and a Frenchman." - David Coleman

~ • ~

"Ten Tour de France riders crashed, two retired after falls, another dropped out when diarrhea slowed him to the point of elimination..." - James Richardson

~ • ~

"It's not only a race against the clock but a race against time itself." - Presenter, BBC Wales

~ • ~

"The Gullikson twins are here. An interesting pair - both of them from Wisconsin." - Dan Maskell

~ • ~

Basketball player Chris Washburn, commenting on his ability to drive to the basket, "Yeah, I can go to my right and my left. That's because I'm amphibious."

"Hollywood is the only place you can wake up in the morning and hear the birds coughing in the trees." - Joe Frisco

~ • ~

"....and that's the world in a nutshell - an appropriate receptacle." - Stan Dunn

~ • ~

"Is this the party to whom I am speaking?" - Lily Tomlin as Ernestine the operator.

~ • ~

"He was an angry man, my Uncle Swanny. He had printed on his grave stone: 'What are you lookin' at?'" - Margaret Smith

~ • ~

"I once wanted to become an atheist, but I gave up - they have no holiday." - Henny Youngman

~ • ~

"Go, and never darken my towels again." - Groucho Marx

~ • ~

"A psychologist once said that we know little about the conscience except that it is soluble in alcohol." - Thomas Blackburn

"I like a woman with a head on her shoulders. I hate necks." - Steve Martin

~ • ~

"No." - President Jimmy Carter's daughter Amy when asked by a reporter if she had any message for the children of America.

~ • ~

"What a hotel we're staying at! The towels are so big and fluffy, you can hardly close your suitcase!" - Bessie and Beulah

~ • ~

"You want something by Bach? Which one, Johann Sebastian or Jacques Offen?" - Victor Borge

~ • ~

"With our first child, I must admit I wasn't prepared for the sticker shock. My wife did all the work, but the hospital still charged us $5,000. I couldn't afford that, so we had to put our daughter on layaway." - Robert G. Lee

~ • ~

A man sits down at a restaurant and looks at the menu. He tells the waiter, "I think I will have the turtle soup."

The waiter leaves, but the man changes his mind to pea soup. He calls out to the waiter, "Excuse me, can you hold the turtle and make it pea?"

"I don't want any yes-men around me. I want everybody to tell me the truth even if it costs them their jobs!" - Sam Goldwyn

~ • ~

"You gotta live somewhere." Motto for Cleveland suggested by Jimmy Brogan.

~ • ~

"Yer beautiful in yer wrath. I shall keep you, and in responding to my passions, yer hatred will kindle into love." - John Wayne as Genghis Khan to Susan Hayward in the movie THE CONQUEROR, 1956

~ • ~

"You just gotta save Christianity, Richard! You just gotta!" - Loretta Young to Richard the Lionhearted in the movie THE CRUSADES, 1935

~ • ~

"Aaeeeyaaayaaaayaayaa!" - Johnny Weissmuller (1904-1984) as Tarzan

~ • ~

"I told you 158 times I cannot stand little notes on my pillow. 'We are out of cornflakes. F.U.' It took me three hours to figure out F.U. was Felix Ungar. It's not your fault Felix: it's a rotten combination, that's all." Walter Matthau to Jack Lemmon in THE ODD COUPLE, 1968

"Dr. Livingstone I Presume. The full name of Dr. Presume." - Unknown

~ • ~

Any child can tell you that the sole purpose of a middle name is so he can tell when he's really in trouble. - Unknown

~ • ~

People who think they know everything are very irritating to those of us who do. - Unknown

~ • ~

"You may already be a loser." - Form letter received by Rodney Dangerfield

~ • ~

"Historical reminder: Always put Horace before Descartes." - Donald O. Rickter

~ • ~

"A doctor can bury his mistakes, but an architect can only advise his client to plant vines." - Frank Lloyd Wright

~ • ~

"I wash everything on the gentle cycle. It's more humane." - Unknown

Worried because they hadn't heard anything for days from the widow in the apartment next door, the mother said to her son, "Tony, would you go next door and see how old Mrs. Pierpoint is?"

A few minutes later, Tony returned.

"Well, is she all right?" asked the mother.

"She's fine, but she's rather annoyed with you," remarked Tony.

"At me?" the mother exclaimed. "Whatever for?"

Tony replied, "Mrs. Pierpoint said it's none of your business how old she is."

~ • ~

Some of the most tactful people on Earth are English. One office supervisor called a secretary in to give her the bad news that she was being fired.

He started the conversation with: "Miss Symthe, I really don't know how we're going to get along without you, but starting Monday, we're going to try."

~ • ~

I love the way everybody is getting fancy job titles. Gas station attendants are now called "petroleum consultants." They saunter over. "I'd recommend the 89 octane unleaded. It's an unpretentious little fuel with a surprising kick. Would you care to sniff the nozzle?" - Robert G. Lee

While carpenters were working outside the old house I had just bought, I busied myself with indoor cleaning. I had just finished washing the floor when one of the workmen asked to use the bathroom.

With dismay I looked from his muddy boots to my newly scrubbed floors. "Just a minute," I said, thinking of a quick solution. "I'll put down newspapers."

"That's all right lady," he responded. "I'm already trained."

~ • ~

"I think a secure profession for young people is a history teacher, because in the future, there will be so much more of it to teach." - Bill Muse

~ • ~

"It is better to keep your mouth closed and let people think you are a fool than to open it and remove all doubt." - Mark Twain

~ • ~

"Once you can accept the universe as matter expanding into nothing that is something, wearing stripes with plaid comes easy." - Albert Einstein

~ • ~

"Careful! We don't want to learn anything from this." - Calvin and Hobbs

"There is nothing wrong with you that reincarnation won't cure." - Jack E. Leonard to Ed Sullivan

~ • ~

After listening to a heated debate over religion a third party was heard to remark, "Thank God I'm an atheist."

~ • ~

A pastor decided to visit his church members one Saturday. At one house it was clear to the pastor that someone was home, but nobody came to the door. The pastor knocked several times and finally took out his card and wrote on the back: "Revelation 3:20 - Behold, I stand at the door and knock. If anyone hears my voice and opens the door, I will come in and dine with him and he with me."

The next day the card showed up in the collection plate. Below the pastor's message was another scripture passage. "Genesis 3:10." Right after the sermon the pastor looked it up and read this passage - "I heard your voice in the garden, and I was afraid because I was naked and I hid myself."

~ • ~

"I remember when I was growing up, a tornado touched down in our neighborhood, uprooting a large tree in the front yard and demolishing the house across the street. Dad went to the door, opened it, surveyed the damage, muttered, 'Damn kids,' and closed the door." - Tim Conway

An American was knocked unconscious in a serious accident while traveling in Australia. The ambulance took him to a local hospital for treatment.

While he finally woke up he asked the nurse, "Was I brought here to die?"

"No love," said the nurse. "You were brought in 'ere yesterday."

~ • ~

"Como frijoles?" (Spanish for 'How have you bean?')

~ • ~

"Opera is when a guy gets stabbed in the back, and instead of bleeding, he sings." - Ed Gardner

~ • ~

"The Vulcan Neck Pinch is not half as powerful as the Vulcan Groin Kick, but it's more politically correct." - William White

~ • ~

"I'm an ordinary sort of fellow - 42 around the chest, 42 around the waist, 96 around the golf course, and a nuisance around the house." - Groucho Marx

~ • ~

"What, me worry?" - Alfred E. Newman

"When compelled to cook, I produce a meal that would make a sword swallower gag." - Russell Baker

~ • ~

"Either this man is dead or my watch has stopped." - Groucho Marx

~ • ~

Robert and Peter had to take an intelligence test as part of a job application. Though both of them found the test a breeze, they admitted to each other that they were stumped by the final question: "Name a 14 letter word for someone in charge of a plant."

"How did you answer that last one?" asked Robert. "I thought it was tough at first....then I thought of Superintendent."

"I got it right too," Pete said. "But I wrote Horticulturist."

~ • ~

"I think the pilot on my last trip was pretty new to his job. I base that on his pre-flight announcement, 'We're going to be taking off in a few... Whoa, here we go!'" - Unknown

~ • ~

"I don't like country music, but I don't mean to denigrate those who do. And for the people who like country music, denigrate means 'put down.'" - Bob Newhart

"Skill without imagination is craftsmanship and gives us many useful objects such as wickerwork picnic baskets. Imagination without skill gives us modern art." - Tom Stoppard, Artist Descending a Staircase, 1972

~ • ~

"Man is the only animal that laughs and has a state legislature." - Samuel Butler (1835-1902)

~ • ~

A rookie police officer was out for his first ride with an experienced partner. A call came in to disperse a group of people who were loitering.

The officers drove to the street and observed a small crowd standing on a corner. The rookie rolled down his window and said, "Let's go people, off the corner."

He got a few glances but no one moved, so he barked again, "I want you off this corner NOW people!"

Intimidated, the people began to leave, casting puzzled stares in his direction.

Proud of the way he handled himself, the young policeman turned to his partner, "Well, how did I do?"

"Pretty good," chuckled the vet, "especially since you just cleared a bus stop."

"He's very, very well known. I'd say he's world-famous in Melbourne." - Dame Edna Everage

~ • ~

"Outside of the killings, Washington has one of the lowest crime rates in the country." - Washington, DC mayor Marion Barry

~ • ~

"I love California. I practically grew up in Phoenix." - Former U.S. vice president Dan Quayle

~ • ~

"The taxpayer - that's someone who works for the Federal Government but doesn't have to take the civil service examination." - Ronald Reagan

~ • ~

"When I finished school, I took one of those career aptitude tests, and based on my verbal ability score, they suggested I become a mime." - Tim Cavanagh

~ • ~

"Remember that as a teenager you are in the last stage of your life in which you will be happy to hear that the phone is for you." - Fran Lebowitz

"You can't go to a public pool and splash around any more. Everyone is swimming laps now. Some guy jumped in behind me and said, "How long you gonna be using this lane, dude?" And I said, "Until my bladder's empty, punk." - Tommy Sledge

~ • ~

"Is my car the only one in America where someone breaks in and turns up my radio every time I park?" - Steven Wright

~ • ~

"That lowdown scoundrel deserves to be kicked to death by a jackass, and I'm just the one to do it." - A Congressional Candidate in Texas

~ • ~

"There are only two truly infinite things, the universe and stupidity. And I am unsure about the universe." - Albert Einstein

~ • ~

"In place of infinity we usually put some really big number, like 15." - Anonymous Computer Science professor

~ • ~

"He grounds the warship he walks on." - John Bracken on Capt. Barney Kelly, who ran the USS Enterprise into the mud of San Francisco Bay in May of 1983.

"Oh, my God - look at you! Anybody else hurt in the accident?"
- Don Rickles to Ernest Borgnine

~ • ~

Now that the metric system is in wide use all over the world, we can see why Americans have not adopted it:

A miss is as good as 1.6 kilometers.
Put your best .3 of a meter forward.
Spare the 5.03 meters and spoil the child.
Twenty-eight grams of prevention is worth 453 grams of cure.
Give a man 2.5 centimeters and he'll take 1.6 kilometers.
Peter Piper picked 8.8 liters of pickled peppers.

~ • ~

Metric Conversion Chart

10**12 microphones = 1 megaphone
10 cards = 1 decacards
10 rations = 1 decoration
10 millipedes = 1 centipede
8 nickles = 2 paradigms
2000 mockingbirds = two kilomockingbirds
453.6 graham crackers = 1 pound cake
3 1/3 tridents = 1 decadent
10 monologs = 5 dialogues
2 monograms = 1 diagram
2 snake eyes = 1 paradise

"To do is to be." - Descartes
"To be is to do." - Voltaire
"Do be do be do." - Frank Sinatra

~ • ~

Chapter Six

Around the Holidays

Dear Yucksters,

PUNXSUTAWNEY, Pa. - For anybody who is completely lost on American tradition, Groundhog Day (February 2) is the time when a furry little marmot is supposed to stick his head out of his hole, look at his shadow and predict whether there will be six more weeks of winter.

The most famous of these weather rodents is Punxsutawney Phil. Every year, in a carnival-like atmosphere, Phil is dragged out of his cage and displayed to thousands of spectators who stand around in the sub-freezing air waiting for his appearance.

It has been over 100 years since German farmers began the festival in Punxsutawney, and it seems to me that it is a very unlikely tradition to start at all. Imagine some poor immigrant trying to feed himself and his family through one of the hardest professions in the world - farming - when suddenly he sees a fat little defenseless creature digging holes in his field.

I would more likely believe an annual groundhog cook-off. But, that's just me. For those of you who didn't catch the news, Phil saw his shadow and predicted six more weeks of winter.

Laugh it up,

Joe

Over breakfast one morning, a woman said to her husband, "I'll bet you don't know what day this is."

"Of course I do," he answered as if he was offended, and left for the office.

At 10:00 a.m., the doorbell rang and when the woman opened the door, she was handed a box of a dozen long-stemmed red roses. At 1:00 p.m., a foil-wrapped, two-pound box of her favorite chocolates was delivered. Later, a boutique delivered a designer dress.

The woman couldn't wait for her husband to come home.

"First the flowers, then the chocolates and then the dress!" she exclaimed. "I've never had a more wonderful Groundhog Day in my life!

~ • ~

This guy goes to a Halloween party with a girl on his back.

"What the heck are you?" asks the host.

"I'm a snail," says the guy.

"But... you have a girl on your back," replies the host.

"Yeah," he says, "that's Michelle!"

[Thanks to Colleen for this gem... which actually gave me night-mares last night. I'll get you Colleen, and your little dog, too!]

Dear Yucksters,

I hope everybody had an exciting and eventful Valentine's Day. I spent a romantic Monday night curled up with a nice glass of wine and the new video release of The 13th Warrior.

I love a good tear-jerker. That scene at the end where the army of cannibal zombies rides down to the fort and Buliwyf the Northman eviscerates the zombie king...it just brings a big lump to my throat...excuse me while I get a tissue.

Laugh it up,

Joe

~ • ~

Earlier today, my girlfriend was brushing some stuff onto her eyelashes that I never saw her wear before. I asked her if she ever used it before, and she said that she used it only once a year. I asked her why, and she said...

"It's my St. Valentine's day mascara."

~ • ~

"It's slim pickings out there. When you're first dating you're so optimistic. At the beginning you're like: I want to meet a guy who's really smart, really sweet, really good-looking, has a really great career.... Eventually you're like: Lord, any mammal with a day job." - Carol Leifer

Dear Yucksters,

I had a fun Easter Sunday. I stopped by my brother Nino's house for brunch (Yes, his real name. My dad was unsympathetic to youthful self-consciousness. If it weren't for my mother he would have saddled me with the name Miro. Thanks, Mom).

Anyhow, Nino had prepared a fully functional omelet bar for our gastronomic pleasure, complete with everything from bacon bits to two different kinds of cheese. All you had to do was yell out the ingredients you wanted and he would whip you up a custom-made omelet.

The only flaw in the operation was that only one person at a time could order an omelet, so not only were we eating in sequence, but poor Nino was kept busy catering to the appetites of fifteen people one by one. By the time I got to the front of the line he just yelled, "Who's next?" and started throwing random ingredients in the pan.

The result was that I got most of whatever ingredient was left - namely onions and freshly chopped jalapenos. When I took that first fiery bite the fumes rose straight to my sinus cavity and snot started running down my nose. I'm not the kind of guy to turn his nose up at a home-made meal, even a runny nose, so I assiduously finished every bite. I can hardly blame the guy. He can pop chilies like beer nuts, so how would he know that he was turning my esophagus into a volcano of sulphurous gas.

In Nino's defense, everyone said that brunch was fantastic. His wife Marianne prepared a honey-baked ham and a beautiful hash-brown casserole, but all I could taste for the rest of the day was jalapenos, so I'll have to take their word for it. Now if you'll excuse me, I have a left-over ham sandwich waiting for me for lunch.

Laugh it up,

Joe

~ • ~

Three blondes found themselves standing before St. Peter at the gate to heaven. St. Peter said to them, "Before you may enter the gates of heaven you have to tell me what Easter is."

The first blonde said, "Easter is a holiday where we all have a big feast and we're thankful."

St. Peter said, "NO! That's Thanksgiving."

The second blonde said, "Easter is a holiday where we celebrate Jesus' birth and give each other presents."

St. Peter said, "NO! That's Christmas."

The third blonde said, "I know what Easter is. Easter is a Christian holiday that coincides with the Jewish festival of Passover. Jesus was having Passover feast with his disciples when he was betrayed by Judas, and the Romans arrested him. The Romans hung him on the cross where he died. Then they buried him in a tomb behind a large boulder."

St. Peter said, "Very good!

Then she adds, "and every year the Jews roll away the boulder and Jesus comes out. If he sees his shadow we have six more weeks of winter."

~ • ~

Dear Yucksters,

It's the tail end of July 4th and I thought I'd stop into the office and drop you a few lines before heading home and turning in for the night. The family threw quite a party this year to celebrate our country's Independence Day. When you come from a family as large as mine everything has to be done on a larger scale than usual.

My cousin Kaz and my brother Nino (no I'm not kidding, those are their names) had three barbeque grills burning simultaneously to feed the crowd that was gathered today. You should have seen the way they deftly organized all that food over multiple heat sources. It almost looked choreographed the way they worked in harmony. That's not something you can learn. You have to be born with that skill.

But before the feast we engaged in several vigorous games of volleyball--a vicious and often merciless sport that results in frequent stubbed toes, jammed fingers and broken pride. Especially when you're playing with my nephews. I remember years ago, we used to play the brothers versus the nephews. The nephews would get a lesson in humility and the brothers would get a little easy exercise to help stimulate the appetite before lunch.

That's not the way it is anymore. Now the brothers are all sedentary and out-of-shape, and the nephews are all broad-shouldered college (and a couple of post-college) athletes. It's a little intimidating when the skinny little kid you used to bean in the head with a volleyball is now six feet, 250 pounds, and spiking the ball at your face. I could almost see the revenge written in his eyes. It seems familial love doesn't reach across a volleyball net.

But, nobody died so all's well that ends well. I just hope I'm able to get out of bed tomorrow morning after all that exercise.

Laugh it up,

Joe

~ • ~

One Halloween a trick-or-treater came to my door dressed as "Rocky", in boxing gloves and satin shorts. Soon after I gave him some goodies, he returned for more.

"Aren't you the same 'Rocky' who left my doorstep a few minutes ago?" I asked.

"Yes," he replied, "but now I'm the sequel. I'll be back three more times tonight, too."

~ • ~

What do you call your girlfriend if she becomes a deer whenever there is a full moon? -- A Were-doe.

When Marco Polo first opened the trade routes to China, he was quite impressed with their rockets. These weren't the fireworks we now know, but they did shoot into the air and explode.

Strangely, no matter where he went, there were people who made fireworks, but he had trouble finding someone to demonstrate them for him.

Then one day Marco came upon an ancient military fortification at the community of Chu'Lai. Here, fireworks were launched every night, and Marco was very impressed!

But still he wondered, "Why here?" At the end of every week, people came from great distances, bringing their own fireworks to launch at the abandoned compound. So Marco Polo asked his guide why everyone should come to this place to launch their fireworks.

Marc's guide replied: "Why honored Sir, We always set off fireworks on the Forts of Chu'Lai."

~ • ~

A little girl was watching her parents dress for a party. When she saw her dad donning his tuxedo, she warned, "Daddy, you shouldn't wear that suit."

"And why not, darling?" He asked.

"You know it always gives you a headache the next morning."

Dear Yucksters,

Monday is Labor Day, when pregnant women all over the United States...er, wait a minute, that's not right. What I wanted to say is that it has something to do with planting trees, but I don't think that's right either.

Alright, alright, here it is...Labor Day is the one day out of the year when U.S. government employees actually work.

Still not buying it, huh? Okay. Labor Day is celebrated in the United States, Puerto Rico, the Canal Zone and the Virgin Islands. We celebrate Labor Day in honor of the working class. It was initiated in the U.S. in 1882 by the Knights of Labor, who held a large parade in New York City for the event. In 1894 the U.S. Congress made the day a legal holiday.

There you have it. And just because we're sympathetic to the working man (hey, we're working men and women ourselves), we're taking the day off as well. So you won't be getting a Clean Laffs issue on Monday. Enjoy the long weekend and I'll see you on Tuesday.

Laugh it up,

Joe

~ • ~

"Blow in its ear." - Johnny Carson on the best way to thaw a frozen turkey.

Dear Yucksters,

Great big gobs of greasy, grimy gopher guts! It's Friday already and I still haven't come up with a costume for Saturday's Halloween party. I'm in a pickle now, but I just might have an idea....I could go as a samurai! No, I'm not Japanese, but I do have a samurai sword.

When I was 15-years-old I decided I wanted to become a martial arts expert (probably after watching a particularly stirring episode of Kung Fu). So instead of wasting time with something trivial like a martial arts school, I pooled my meagar resources and invested in a thirty-one-inch tongue of gleaming death. Boy, was I impressed with myself. I was a man, no....I was more. I was a steely-eyed warrior ready to dispense the killing stroke with the elegant but deadly weapon of the ancient bushi.

All I had to do was get the sword into the house without Dad seeing it. If he saw what I had blown all my cash on he would have killed me. I practiced with that thing for, boy, it must have been two or three hours before it found a permanent resting place in a closet. But now, at long last, owning that stupid thing is finally going to pay off. It's the perfect cornerstone on which to build a killer costume.

All I need now is a pair of those baggy pants you see guys wearing in martial arts movies, a kimono and a pair of those zori sandals. An investment of an additional couple hundred dollars should do it. I'll let you know how the party goes next week.

Laugh it up,

Joe

A pirate walks off his ship. He has a wooden leg, a hook for a hand, and a patch over his right eye. He sits down on a bench, and begins throwing peanuts to the seagulls.

Two curious young children shyly sit down next to him and ask the pirate how he came to have a wooden leg.

The pirate replies, "Well, I was standing on the deck of me ship one day, and a wave washed me overboard. Then, a hungry shark attacked me and bit me leg off."

The little boy then asks, "How did you lose your hand?"

"Many years ago, I was fighting the Navy, and one of them boys cut me hand off. Me doc couldn't find a hand, so he gave me this hook."

Next, the little girl asks, "How did you lose your eye?"

"Well, I was standing watch up in the crow's nest, and just as I looked up, a lousy seagull flew over and did his business right in me eye."

The children, now thoroughly confused, ask, "How did that cause you to lose your eye?"

The pirate explains, "Well, it was me first day with the hook..."

~ • ~

A skeleton walks into a bar and says to the bartender, "Give me a beer and a mop."

Dear Yucksters,

It's two days 'til turkey and I've already started fasting so my appetite will have a keen edge for the feast. For any non-U.S. residents who might not know what old Joe is talking about, I'm referring to the venerable tradition of Thanksgiving and the frenzy of feasting it inspires. Let me give you a brief overview and history of this important holiday to help you understand the mania we experience every year.

Thanksgiving celebrates the pilgrims' first successful year in the New World (that's North America to you). The pilgrims came to America seeking religious freedom and settled in Plymouth in 1620.

The first year didn't go so well, and after a brutal winter spent eating tree bark and the occasional frozen squirrel, the pilgrims were getting a little dissatisfied with their new home.

Then, in the Spring of 1621, they met a native American named Squanto who noticed the poor foreigners had the survival skills of a carton of unrefrigerated milk. Squanto had traveled to England and learned the language, so he took it upon himself to teach the pilgrims the fundamentals of agriculture, and that not everything they found lying in the forest was good to eat.

By the Fall of that year the settlers were swimming in grits, and to celebrate, the pilgrim governor Bill Bradford threw a swinging gig and invited all his new friends. And that's the beginning of Thanksgiving.

So you see, to remind ourselves of starvation narrowly averted we stuff ourselves to the point of discomfort every year. It's a very important holiday in America. About the only Americans who don't enjoy it are the turkeys. But we still invite them every year.

Laugh it up,

Joe

~ • ~

During a radio interview an American and a UK journalist were discussing Thanksgiving. The American asked if we celebrated Thanksgiving in the UK.

"Yes," the Brit replied, "but we celebrate it on the 6th of September."

"Why then?"

"That's when they left."

~ • ~

Dear Yucksters,

Being the bachelor in the family has its advantages and its disadvantages. Mostly it has disadvantages. For instance: Thanksgiving dinner. You see, all of my siblings already have their own kids. So when they make up their guest lists they always think in families. "We could invite Paul and his family," or "Loretta and her family," or "Michael and his family." Poor old Joe is usually an afterthought.

Another contributing factor is that everybody still thinks I'm seven years old. It's a symptom of being the youngest. The consequence of this delusion is that I'm usually invited at the last minute and seated in places like the piano bench, or the folding table in the kitchen or in the basement at the washing machine.

And turkey pickings get mighty slim when you're seated at the washing machine. I remember one year I got a neck bone. Because there's a hierarchy for Thanksgiving dinner and I am not in an advantageous position. Dad gets first crack and he waits right by the oven. By the time the bird reaches the table the poor sucker is missing most of the skin off its back. It tends to diminish the presentation, but Dad will not be denied.

And it goes down the line, with the best bits getting picked off first. Not to say that there isn't an abundance of food. The table is usually adorned with a ham, or a pork roast, or maybe even an entire roast beef, but there's only one turkey and it goes fast.

Some of my older nephews also get the bachelor treatment and one of them shared his secret technique with me. He said that he goes to his girlfriend's house for an early Thanksgiving dinner, and his "guest" status earns him a much better seat at the table than his "oldest son" status earns him at home. The little sneak. But I'm not complaining (much), because despite it all Thanksgiving is still the best tasting holiday of the year.

Laugh it up,

Joe

A Sunday School teacher read a passage from the Old Testament book of Jonah to her class:

"And the Lord appointed a great fish to swallow up Jonah; and Jonah was in the belly of the fish three days and three nights. Then Jonah prayed to the Lord his God from the belly of the fish, saying 'I called to the Lord out of my distress and He answered me.' ...and the Lord spoke to the fish, and it vomited out Jonah upon the dry land." (Jonah 1:17)

When she had finished reading, the teacher said, "Now, children, you have heard the Bible story of Jonah and the whale. What does this story teach us?"

One ten-year-old shouted, "You can't keep a good man down!"

~ • ~

Santa Claus, like all pilots, gets regular visits by an examiner from the Federal Aviation Administration.

The examiner walked slowly around the sled. He checked the reindeer harnesses, the landing gear, and Rudolph's nose. He painstakingly reviewed Santa's weight and balance calculations for the sled's enormous payload.

Finally, they were ready for the checkride. Santa got in and fastened his seatbelt and then the examiner hopped in carrying, to Santa's surprise, a shotgun.

"What's that for?" asked Santa incredulously.

The examiner winked and said, "I'm not supposed to tell you this, but you're gonna lose an engine on takeoff."

Chapter Seven

Stories, Lists & Narratives

Dear Yucksters,

I was digging through my assets the other day (I'm the kind of guy who has assets you can dig through) when I happened across a battered old box full of class notes from years and years ago. A whole stack of spiral notebooks full of scribbles on everything from Music Appreciation to Physics.

I spent an hour sitting in the storage closet poring over my now nearly indecipherable notes, and it occurred to me that the entire, musty, yellowing stack of paper was completely worthless. If I had ever known what Tutti Allegro means, or cared about Endoplasmic Reticulum, I didn't now. So why have these echoes of academia been following me around the country for the past eight years?

Maybe it's the simple volume of work I put into writing them, or maybe it's guilt over the fact that I only retained about four percent of my education. But keeping all this material seemed like an unnatural attachment, so as an experiment I tried to destroy one. I picked up Biology 101 and tried to tear it in half - but I couldn't bring myself to do it! My conscience just wouldn't bear it.

So now I have this indestructible library of nostalgia that is doomed to follow me around from place to place forever. They'll end up burying me in some distant future with my college biology notes and my high school letterman jacket. Has anyone else experienced this? Is there a way to exorcise this unreasonable attachment to the past? I'm willing to listen to any suggestions as long as they don't involve hiring hypnotists or any kind of arson. In the meantime I'll be trying to figure out what a phagocyte is.

Laugh it up,

Joe

~ • ~

The Pope just finished a tour of the East Coast and was taking a limousine to the airport. Since he'd never driven a limo, he asked the chauffeur if he could drive for a while.

The reluctant chauffeur pulled over along the roadside, climbed into the back of the limo, and the Pope took the wheel. The Pope then merged onto the highway and accelerated to over 90 mph to see what the limo could do.

Suddenly, the Pope noticed the blue light of the State Patrol in his side mirror, so he pulled over.

The trooper approached the limo, peered in through the windows, then said, "Just a moment please, I need to call in."

The trooper called in and explained to the chief that he had a very important person pulled over for speeding. "How do I handle this, chief?" asked the trooper.

"Is it the Governor?" questioned the chief.

"No! This guy is even more important!"

"Is it the President?" asked the chief.

"No! Even more important!"

"Well, who the heck is it?" screamed the chief.

"I don't know, sir," replied the trooper, "but he's got the Pope as his chauffeur."

~ • ~

The manager of a large city zoo was drafting a letter to order a pair of animals. He sat at his computer and typed the following sentence: "I would like to place an order for two mongooses, to be delivered at your earliest convenience."

He stared at the screen, focusing on that odd word 'mongooses'. Then he deleted the word and added another, so that the sentence now read: "I would like to place an order for two mongeese, to be delivered at your earliest convenience."

Again he stared at the screen, this time focusing on the new word, which seemed just as odd as the original one. Finally, he deleted the whole sentence and started all over. "Everyone knows no fully-stocked zoo should be without a mongoose," he typed. "Please send us two of them."

The US Federal Aviation Administration has a unique device for testing the strength of windshields on airplanes. The device is a gun that launches a dead chicken at a plane's windshield at approximately the speed the plane flies.

The theory is that if the windshield doesn't crack from the carcass impact, it'll survive a real collision with a bird during flight. It seems the British were very interested in this and wanted to test a windshield on a brand new, speedy locomotive they're developing.

They borrowed the FAA's chicken launcher, loaded the chicken and fired. The ballistic chicken shattered the windshield, went through the engineer's chair, broke an instrument panel and embedded itself in the back wall of the engine cab. The British were stunned and asked the FAA to recheck the test to see if everything was done correctly.

The FAA reviewed the test thoroughly and only had one recommendation: "Use a thawed chicken."

~ • ~

The worried housewife sprang to the telephone when it rang and listened with relief to the kindly voice in her ear.

"How are you, darling?" it said. "What kind of a day are you having?"

"Oh, mother," said the housewife, breaking into bitter tears, "I've had such a bad day. The baby won't eat and the washing machine broke down. I haven't had a chance to go shopping, and besides, I've just sprained my ankle and I have to hobble around. On top of that, the house is a mess and I'm supposed to have two couples to dinner tonight."

The mother was shocked and was at once all sympathy. "Oh, darling," she said, "sit down, relax, and close your eyes. I'll be over in half an hour. I'll do your shopping, clean up the house, and cook your dinner for you. I'll feed the baby and I'll call a repairman I know who'll be at your house to fix the washing machine promptly. Now stop crying. I'll do everything. In fact, I'll even call George at the office and tell him he ought to come home and help out for once."

"George?" said the housewife. "Who's George?"

"Why, George! Your husband!....Is this 223-1374?"

"No, this is 223-1375."

"Oh, I'm sorry. I guess I have the wrong number."

There was a short pause and the housewife said in a small voice, "Does this mean you're not coming over?"

~ • ~

An older couple had a son, who was still living with them. The parents were a little worried, as the son was unable to decide about his future career... so they decided to do a small test.

They took a ten-dollar bill, a Bible, and a bottle of whiskey, and put them on the front hall table. Then they hid in the closet, pretending they were not at home. The father's plan was: "If our son takes the money, he will be a businessman, if he takes the Bible, he will be a priest - but if he takes the bottle of whiskey, I'm afraid our son will be a drunkard."

Peeping through the keyhole they saw their son arrive... he slid the ten-dollar bill in his pocket. He flipped through the Bible, and took it. Finally he grabbed the bottle, and took an appreciative whiff, then he left for his room, carrying all three items.

The father slapped his forehead, and said: "It's even worse than I could have imagined. Our son is going to be a politician!"

~ • ~

Science has a language of its own which sometimes puzzles laymen. The word "obvious" is a case in point.

A professor of physics, deriving some profound theory for the class, scribbled an equation on the board and said, "From this, it is obvious that we can proceed to the following relationship..." and he scribbled a second and equally long equation.

Then he paused. He stared hard at the two equations and said, "Wait a minute, I may be wrong..."

He sat down and began to write at his desk furiously, crossing out and rewriting for five minutes while the class sat in absolute silence waiting for the verdict.

Finally, the professor rose with an air of satisfaction and said, "Yes, I was right in the first place. It *IS* obvious that the second equation follows from the first."

MARRIAGES MADE IN HEAVEN ???

If Yoko Ono married Sonny Bono, she'd be Yoko Ono Bono.

If Dolly Parton married Salvador Dali, she'd be Dolly Dali.

If Bo Derek married Don Ho, she'd be Bo Ho.

If Oprah Winfrey married Deepak Chopra, she'd be Oprah Chopra.

If Olivia Newton-John married Wayne Newton, then divorced him to marry Elton John, she'd be Olivia Newton-John Newton John.

If Sondra Locke married Elliott Ness, then divorced him to marry Herman Munster, she'd become Sondra Locke Ness Munster.

If Bea Arthur married Sting, she'd be Bea Sting.

If Liv Ullman married Judge Lance Ito, then divorced him and married Jerry Mathers, she'd be Liv Ito Beaver.

If Snoop Doggy Dogg married Winnie the Pooh, he'd be Snoop Doggy Dogg Pooh.

If G. Gordon Liddy married Boutros-Boutros Ghali, then divorced him to marry Kenny G., he'd be G. Ghali G.

~ • ~

[After the success of yesterday's marriage quips I was happy to stumble on these unlikely corporate mergers.]

1. Hale Business Systems, Mary Kay Cosmetics, Fuller Brush, and W.R. Grace Company merge to become...Hale Mary Fuller Grace.

2. Polygram Records, Warner Brothers, and Keebler Crackers merge to become...Polly-Warner-Cracker.

3. 3M and Goodyear merge to become...MMM Good.

4. John Deere and Abitibi-Price merge to become...Deere Abi.

5. Zippo Manufacturing, Audi Motors, Dofasco, and Dakota Mining merge to become...Zip Audi Do Da.

6. Honeywell, Imasco, and Home Oil merge to become... Honey I'm Home.

7. Denison Mines, and Alliance and Metal Mining merge to become...Mine-All-Mine.

8. Federal Express and UPS merge to become...FED UP.

9. Fairchild Electronics and Honeywell Computers will merge and become...Fairwell Honeychild.

~ • ~

A man had been driving all night and by morning was still far from his destination. He decided to stop at the next city he came to, and park somewhere quiet so he could get an hour or two of sleep.

As luck would have it, the quiet place he chose happened to be on one of the city's major jogging routes. No sooner had he settled back to snooze when there came a knocking on his window. He looked out and saw a jogger running in place.

"Yes?"

"Excuse me, sir," the jogger said, "do you have the time?"

The man looked at the car clock and answered, "8:15." The jogger said thanks and left. The man settled back again, and was just dozing off when there was another knock on the window and another jogger.

"Excuse me, sir, do you have the time?"

"8:25!" The jogger said thanks and left. Now the man could see other joggers passing by and he knew it was only a matter of time before another one disturbed him. To avoid the problem, he got out a pen and paper and put a sign in his window saying, "I do not know the time!"

Just as he was dozing off once again there was another knock on the window. "Sir, sir? It's 8:45!"

~ • ~

A preacher, who was "humor impaired," attended a conference to help encourage and better equip pastors for their ministry.

Among the speakers were many well known and dynamic speakers. One such boldly approached the pulpit and, gathering the entire crowd's attention, said, "The best years of my life were spent in the arms of a woman that wasn't my wife!" The crowd was shocked! He followed up by saying, "And that woman was my mother!" The crowd burst into laughter and delivered the rest of his talk, which went over quite well.

The next week, our pastor decided he'd give this humor thing a try, and use that joke in his sermon. As he approached the pulpit that Sunday, he tried to rehearse the joke in his head. It suddenly seemed a bit foggy to him.

Getting to the microphone he said loudly, "The greatest years of my life were spent in the arms of a woman that was not my wife!" The congregation inhaled in surprise. After standing there for almost 10 seconds in the stunned silence, trying to recall the second half of the joke, the pastor finally blurted out, "...and I can't remember who she was!"

~ • ~

READ THE SIGNS:

On an Electrician's truck: "Let us remove your shorts."

Outside a Radiator Repair Shop: "Best place in town to take a leak."

In a Non-smoking area: "If we see you smoking we will assume you are on fire and take appropriate action."

On a Maternity Room door: "Push, Push, Push."

At an Optometrist's Office: "If you don't see what you're looking for, you've come to the right place."

At a Car Dealership: "The best way to get back on your feet - miss a car payment."

Outside a Muffler Shop: "No appointment necessary. We'll hear you coming."

Outside a Hotel: "Help! We need inn-experienced people."

At an Auto Body Shop: "May we have the next dents?"

In a Dry Cleaner's Emporium: "Drop your pants here."

In a Veterinarian's office: "Be back in 5 minutes. Sit! Stay!"

On a Music Teacher's door: "Out Chopin."

At the Electric Company: "We would be delighted if you send in your bill. However, if you don't, you will be."

On the side of a Garbage Truck: "We've got what it takes to take what you've got."

In a Restaurant window: "Don't stand there and be hungry, come in and get fed up."

Inside a Bowling Alley: "Please be quiet. We need to hear a pin drop."

Dear Yucksters,

When I set my mind to something I do it. So like I promised, I went bike shopping this weekend. I have to tell you, it was exciting and scary all at the same time.

I've heard some good things about Suzuki, so I went to one of their dealerships and asked the guy what he recommended. He looked me over with an appraising eye and said, "I've got THE bike for you, Joe. Come on over here and take a look at the brand-new 2000 Savage."

I liked it already. The 2000 Savage. That was me alright. But when we walked into the showroom and actually stood in front of the thing I was transfixed. It was all yellow and black, like a giant bumblebee, except with a chrome-plated exhaust pipe.

"This is a good bike for an inexperienced rider," the salesman said. "It's only 352 pounds, which makes it very easy to maneuver, but trust me, the 652 cc single cylinder will give you all the low end torque you can handle."

Yeah. Low end torque. That's what I need.

"It's got an air-cooled engine with a compression ratio of 8 to 5 to 1, a single over-head cam and 5-speed transmission."

Yeah. A compression ratio. That's what I need.

"And you want to talk about comfort? It's got an oil damped, telescopic coil spring in front, and a twin shock, 5-way adjustable spring in back. Plus, a clean-running belt drive for exceptionally smooth operation."

Yeah. Telescopic, 5-way adjustable belt drive.

"Now, Joe," continued the salesman, "You might think that a bike like this is too..."

"I'll take it," I interrupted.

"You'll take it?"

"I'll take it."

"Excellent!" he said. Sensing the sale was a matter of timing, he quickly ushered me over to his desk before the euphoria wore off.

"Let me see now, the MSRP, plus doc fee, prep fee, tax, tag, title, and the finance charge, of course, ha-ha-ha..."

He was scribbling furiously while I looked wide-eyed through a catalog of options.

"That will come tooo....ahhhh....one hundred and seventy beans a month. That's assuming a minimum down-payment, of course, ha-ha-ha!"

"Ha-ha-ha," I answered, "Tell me, you got any used bikes?"

Do you ever notice how salespeople have really severe mood swings?

Laugh it up,

Joe

Dear Yucksters,

Well, the system has finally and conclusively failed. The state of Illinois has given me a Class D motorcycle license. I have to say, I thought the whole procedure was going to be a lot harder than it actually was. The woman at the DMV said that half the applicants have to take the written test at least twice before they pass. After hearing that I was expecting a ten-page essay exam on everything from vehicle safety legislation to the history of the internal combustion engine. What I got was 15 multiple choice questions along the lines of:

"If you are riding in heavy traffic and the vehicles ahead of you begin to slow down suddenly, do you:

a) Firmly apply both the front and rear brakes at the same time while quickly looking for an escape route from traffic.

b) Let go of the handle bars, cover your eyes and pray for a quick death.

c) Lay the bike down and try to slide under a gas truck like Arnold Schwarzenegger in Terminator II."

Passing the written exam earned me a learner's permit. That's a little slip of paper that gives you permission to tool around the neighborhood annoying old folks and terrorizing dogs. I did that for two weeks until my big riding skills test a few days ago.

Now that was hard. They assigned a little old man to test me and he seemed none too happy to be standing out on the windy parking lot at eight o'clock in the morning. He stood in the middle of a painted box about twice the size of a parking space and had me perform a series of maneuvers around him like a U-turn, a figure eight and a mobius circle, all the while screaming instructions and criticism at the top of his lungs.

"Now brake! Now accelerate! Watch out for the cones! TURN for cryin' out loud, TURN!"

At the end of it all he peered over the top of his trifocals and ticked the box marked "Pass" and said, "Try not to kill yourself, kid." That was it. I was a licensed motorcyclist. It was a little anticlimactic, actually. Now, I've got to rent some good motor-cycle movies. Anybody remember C.C. Ryder with Joe Namath?

Laugh it up,

Joe

~ • ~

We've all heard of the Air Force's high-security, super-secret base in Nevada, known simply as "Area 51?"

Late one afternoon, the Air Force folks out at Area 51 were very surprised to see a Cessna landing at their "secret" base. They immediately impounded the aircraft and hauled the pilot into an interrogation room.

The pilot's story was that he took off from Las Vegas, got lost, and spotted the Base just as he was about to run out of fuel. The Air Force started a full FBI background check on the pilot and held him overnight during the investigation.

By the next day, they were finally convinced that the pilot really was lost and wasn't a spy. They gassed up his airplane, gave him a terrifying 'you-did-not-see-a-base' briefing, complete with threats of spending the rest of his life in prison, told him Las Vegas was that-a-way on such-and-such a heading, and sent him on his way.

The next day, to the total disbelief of the Air Force, the same Cessna showed up again. Once again, the MPs surrounded the plane...only this time there were two people in the plane.

The same pilot jumped out and said, "Do anything you want to me, but my wife is in the plane and you have to tell her where I was last night!"

~ • ~

[Don't know if this one's true, but it sounds like something a lawyer would do....]

A New Orleans lawyer sought an FHA loan for a client. He was told the loan would be granted if he could prove satisfactory title to a parcel of property being offered as collateral. The title to the property dated back to 1803, which took the lawyer three months to track down.

After sending the information to the FHA, he received the following reply:

"Upon review of your letter adjoining your client's loan application, we note that the request is supported by an Abstract of Title. While we compliment the able manner in which you have prepared and presented the application, we must point out that you have only cleared title to the proposed collateral proper back to 1803. Before final approval can be accorded, it will be necessary to clear the title back to its origin."

Annoyed, the lawyer responded as follows:

"Your letter regarding title in Case No. 189156 has been received. I note that you wish to have title extended further than the 194 years covered by the present application. I was unaware that any educated person in this country, particularly those working in the property area, could not know that Louisiana was purchased by the U.S. from France in 1803, the year of origin identified in our application.

For the edification of uninformed FHA bureaucrats, the title to the land prior to U.S. ownership was obtained from France, which had acquired it by Right of Conquest from Spain. The land came into possession of Spain by Right of Discovery made in the year 1492 by a sea captain named Christopher Columbus, who had been granted the privilege of seeking a new route to India by the then reigning monarch, Isabella. The good queen, being a pious woman and careful about titles, almost as much as the FHA, took the precaution of securing the blessing of the Pope before she sold her jewels to fund the expedition.

Now the Pope, as I'm sure you know, is an emissary of Jesus Christ, the Son of God. And God, it is commonly accepted, created this world. Therefore, I believe it is safe to presume that He also made that part of the world called Louisiana. He, therefore, would be the owner of origin. I hope to hell you find his original claim to be satisfactory. Now, may we have our loan?"

Actual Answering Machine Messages Recorded and Verified By The World Famous International Institute of Answering Machine Messages:

10. My wife and I can't come to the phone right now, but if you'll leave your name and number, we'll get back to you as soon as we're finished.

9. Hello, you are talking to a machine. I am capable of receiving messages. My owners do not need siding, windows or a hot tub, and their carpets are clean. They give to charity at the office and don't need their picture taken. If you're still with me, leave your name and home phone number and they will get back to you.

8. This is not an answering machine - this is a telepathic thought-recording device. After the tone, think about your name, your number, and your reason for calling.... and I'll think about returning your call.

7. Hi! John's answering machine is broken. This is his refrigerator. Please speak very slowly, and I'll stick your message to myself with one of these magnets.

6. Hi. This is John: If you are the phone company, I already sent the money. If you are my parents, please send money. If you are my bank, you didn't lend me enough money. If you are my friends, you owe me money. If you are a female, don't worry, I have LOTS of money.

5. A is for academics, B is for beer. One of those reasons is why we're not here. So, leave a message.

4. Hello! If you leave a message, I'll call you soon. If you leave a "sexy" message, I'll call sooner.

3. Hi. Now YOU say something.

2. Hi. I'm probably home, I'm just avoiding someone I don't like. Leave me a message, and if I don't call back, it's you.

And the Number 1 Actual Answering Machine Message Recorded and Verified by The World Famous International Institute of Answering Machine Messages.

1. Hello, you've reached Jim and Sonya. We can't pick up the phone right now, because we're doing something we really enjoy. Sonya likes doing it up and down, and I like doing it left to right... real slowly. So leave a message, and when we're done brushing our teeth, we'll call you back.

~ • ~

[English is a tricky language. Especially when you're using it in a translation. Following are a few English signs that have been observed in public places around the world. I think they illustrate the point quite elegantly....]

"Is forbitten to steal hotel towels please. If you are not person to do such thing is please not to read notice." - In a Tokyo Hotel

"The lift is being fixed for the next day. During that time we regret that you will be unbearable." - In a Bucharest Hotel Lobby

"To move the cabin, push button for wishing floor. If the cabin should enter more persons, each one should press a number of wishing floor. Driving is then going alphabetically by national order." - In a Belgrade Hotel Elevator

"Please leave your values at the front desk." - In a Paris Hotel Elevator

"The flattening of underwear with pleasure is the job of the chambermaid." - In a Yugoslavian Hotel

"You are invited to take advantage of the chambermaid." - In a Japanese Hotel

"Not to perambulate the corridors in the hours of repose in the boots of ascension." - In an Austrian hotel catering to skiers

"Our wines leave you nothing to hope for." - On the Menu of a Swiss Restaurant

"Special today---no ice cream." - In a Swiss mountain inn

"Special cocktails for the ladies with nuts." - In a Tokyo bar

"When passenger of foot heave in sight, tootle the horn. Trumpet him melodiously at first, but if he still obstacles your passage then tootle him with vigor." - From a brochure of a car rental firm in Tokyo

And finally, an English translation of a Russian translation of the popular English phrase - Out of sight, out of mind. "Invisible Insanity."

Dear Yucksters,

Pardon me if my thoughts seem a little incoherent today. I'm still coming down from a buzz I got on Monday. I finally finished the painting project I started a couple weeks ago and those paint fumes can be a little dangerous.

It wouldn't have been such a hazardous task if I wasn't locked in that room with a gallon of high gloss Acrylic. But it was a necessity. You see, the guy who lived in the apartment before me was insane. He covered half the room with wood paneling and crown molding. And then, to add insult to injury, he painted all the wood; even the doors themselves, baby blue. And really, the only thing to cover a painted wood surface is an oil-based paint. You've just got to be careful of those fumes.

So after days of sanding and priming all of that depressing blue paint I was finally ready to apply my finish coat. Of course, I had to pick a nice 90 degree day to do it on. It was so hot in there the paint was practically drying on the brush. The only thing to do was to close the window and turn on the air-conditioning. Then the only thing missing was a little Jimi Hendrix music. Excuse me while I kiss the sky...or floor, for that matter. I practically passed out after 30 minutes. It took me ten hours to paint 180 square feet because of all the breaks I had to take.

But, at least it's done. And now I have a pristine, glossy white bedroom. Actually, it sort of looks like an operating theater. I'm afraid to sleep in there. Maybe I'll just move a desk and chair in and call it an office.

Laugh it up,

Joe

A Scout Master was teaching his boys about survival in the desert. "What are the three most important things you should bring with you in case you get lost in the desert?" he asked.

Several hands went up, and many good ideas were suggested such as food, matches, etc.

Then one little boy in the back eagerly raised his hand. "Yes Timmy, what are the three most important things you would bring with you?" asked the Scout Master.

Timmy replied: "A compass, a canteen of water, and a deck of cards."

"Why's that Timmy?"

"Well," answered Timmy, "the compass is to find the right direction, the water is to prevent dehydration..."

"And what about the deck of cards?" asked the Scout Master.

"Well, Sir, as soon as you start playing Solitaire, someone is bound to come up behind you and say, "Put that red nine on top of that black ten!"

~ • ~

Two elderly ladies from Boston found themselves in Los Angeles one day in late September when the warm season was at its very warmest and the temperature had reached above the one hundred degree mark.

"Heavens, Louise," said one. "It is certainly very hot here."

"Ah, yes," said the other. "But then, we must remember that we are fully three thousand miles from the ocean."

~ • ~

A young girl who was writing a paper for school came to her father and asked, "Dad, what is the difference between anger and exasperation?"

The father replied, "It is mostly a matter of degree. Let me show you what I mean."

With that the father went to the telephone and dialed a number at random. To the man who answered the phone, he said, "Hello, is Melvin there?"

The man answered, "There is no one living here named Melvin. Why don't you learn to look up numbers before you dial them?"

"See," said the father to his daughter. "That man was not a bit happy with our call. Now watch...."

The father dialed the number again. "Hello, is Melvin there?" asked the father.

"Now look here!" came the heated reply. "You just called this number and I told you that there is no Melvin here! You've got a lot of nerve calling again!" The receiver slammed down hard.

The father turned to his daughter and said, "You see, that was anger. Now I'll show you what exasperation means."

He dialed the same number, and when a violent voice roared, "Hello!" the father calmly said, "Hello, this is Melvin. Have there been any calls for me?"

[As always, I cannot verify the authenticity of any story sent to me...but this one kind of smacks of realism, doesn't it?]

Last summer, down on Lake Isabella, located in the high desert, an hour east of Bakersfield, a blonde, new to boating was having a problem. No matter how hard she tried, she just couldn't get her brand new 22-ft Bayliner to perform. It wouldn't get on a plane at all, and it was very sluggish in almost every maneuver, no matter how much power she applied.

After about an hour of trying to make it go, she putted over to a nearby marina. Maybe they could tell her what was wrong. A thorough topside check revealed everything was in perfect working order. The engine ran fine, the outdrive went up and down, and the prop was the correct size and pitch.

So, one of the marina guys jumped in the water to check underneath the boat. He came up choking on water, he was laughing so hard.

Under the boat, still strapped securely in place, was the trailer.

~ • ~

Chapter Eight

Guaranteed to Roll Your Eyes

Dear Yucksters,

I'd like to focus today on one of my favorite forms of humor: the pun. Of all word play it's the most insidious. Attacking your phunny bone like a virus, the joke creeps up on you until your eyes roll back and a pained groan escapes your lips as the punchline finally hits. And despite all that something still makes you tell it to your friends. You can't help it, you have to share the punishment (groan).

Following are a few polished pearls I've painstakingly picked for your perusal. If you find that it's too much for you to stand alone feel free to forward this to a friend. Just make sure it's a good friend because jokes like these could easily alienate a casual acquaintence.

Laugh it up,

Joe

~ • ~

A termite walks into a bar room and asks, "Is the bar tender here?"

A professor of Greek takes his torn suit to a Greek tailor. The tailor looks at the pants and says, "Euripides?"

"Yes," replies the professor, "Eumenides?"

~ • ~

"I would like to reaffirm my belief in Buddha," Said the monk, "but there is a great deal to be said for margarine."

~ • ~

The next time you're feeling down remember... if the world didn't suck, we'd all fall off.

~ • ~

Q: What do you get when you cross the Godfather with a lawyer?

A: An offer you can't understand.

~ • ~

"This morning I felt that today was going to be my lucky day. I got up at seven, had seven dollars in my pocket, there were seven of us at lunch and there were seven horses in the seven o'clock race - so I backed the seventh."

"Did he win?"

"No, he came in seventh."

Two servicemen in Africa are bragging about who is the better lion hunter. They bet a pint of beer on who will be the first to bag his game.

The first man sets out on foot while the second sneaks off to the nearby air base where he borrows a fighter plane. The man in the plane soon sights a lion and shoots it.

Later, as he displays his prize, the winner points out to his friend that a strafed lion is the shortest distance between two pints.

~ • ~

An electric eel was becoming very depressed, and his keeper asked if there was anything he could do.

"Well, it's getting a little lonely in here," said the eel.

So the next day the keeper dropped a female eel into the tank, but after swimming around a bit the male was just as depressed.

"What's the matter now," asked the keeper.

The eel gestured to his new tank mate and in a tone of resignation said, "DC."

~ • ~

Q: What's the difference between a cat and a comma?

A: A cat has its claws at the end of its paws and a comma has its pause at the end of a clause.

A group of bats, hanging at the ceiling of a cave, discovers a single bat STANDING upright underneath on the floor of the cave. Surprised by this unusual behavior, they ask this fellow: "What the hell are you doing down there?"

And the fellow shouts back: "Yoga!"

~ • ~

Complained the rebellious young kitten to its parents, "Why won't you let me lead my own lives?"

~ • ~

Four men were in a boat. While they were sailing they decided to have a cigarette, but soon discovered that no one had any matches. Finally, one of the sailors came up with a solution. He threw one cigarette overboard. This worked well. They were able to smoke, because the boat had become a cigarette lighter.

~ • ~

Q: So did you hear about the new Pirate movie?

A: It's rated... Arrrrgh!!!

~ • ~

A man goes into a pet store and asks the clerk, "Do you have any dogs that go cheap?"

The salesman says, "No, we have birds that go cheep. Our dogs go BARK!"

"Living on Earth is expensive, but it does include a free trip around the sun." - Unknown

~ • ~

Is "person-person" the politically correct term for mailman?

~ • ~

Two bees buzz around what's left of a rose bush. "How was your summer?" Bee #1 asks.

"Not too good," says Bee #2. "Lotta rain, lotta cold. Not enough flowers, not enough pollen."

The first bee has an idea. "Hey, why don't you go down to the corner and hang a left? There's a bar mitzvah going on. Plenty of flowers and fruit."

Bee #2 buzzes, "Thanks!" and takes off.

An hour later, the bees bump into each other again. "How was the bar mitzvah?" asks Bee #1.

"Great!" says Bee #2.

The first bee peers at his pal and wonders, "What's that on your head?"

"A yarmulke," is the answer. "I didn't want them to think I was a wasp."

The insurance agent was questioning a cowboy who had applied for a policy. "Ever have an accident?" he inquired.

"Nope," was the answer.

"Not even one?" asked the agent incredulously.

"Nope," the cowboy insisted. "Rattler bit me once, though."

"And don't you call that an accident?" exclaimed the agent.

"Nope; the danged varmint done it a-purpose."

~ • ~

186,000 miles/sec: It's not just a good idea, it's the LAW!

~ • ~

What did the elephant say to the naked man?

"It's cute... but can it pick up peanuts?"

~ • ~

We have an old tree that became diseased and was losing its bark. We felt it needed a bark transplant and called a tree surgeon for the job. The message was misread and when the surgeon arrived, he went to work on a tree across the street.

He was halfway done when I noticed the error. I tried to stop him, yelling, "Stop! Stop! You're barking up the wrong tree!"

Dear Yucksters,

Well, I've been working too hard. When the alarm clock went off this morning I got up, walked over to the dresser and grabbed a box of cotton swabs sitting next to the clock. I then spent a full sixty seconds dragging the "Q-Tips" around the dresser top while I stared intently at the digital clock face trying to click the icon that would turn the alarm off.

I've got to take an asprin now.

Laugh it up,

Joe

~ • ~

Tarzan and Jane were expecting their fourth child and were pretty strapped for cash, so Tarzan decided to go into the used-crocodile business. Monday morning he got up early, put on his best loin cloth, swung down to the river, and spent the whole day fighting, haggling over and hassling with cranky crocs.

As dusk fell, a wan Tarzan swung back to the treehouse and demanded, "Quick, Jane, a martini!" Tossing it back he barked, "Another, Jane, make it a double!" Gulping it down, he held out his glass again. "One more, Jane."

"Aw, honey, don't you think you're overdoing it a bit?" she chided gently.

"You don't understand, Jane... it's a jungle out there."

A man approached a local in a village he was visiting. "What's the quickest way to York?"

The local scratched his head. "Are you walking or driving?"

"I'm driving," the stranger answered.

"Well, That's the quickest way!"

~ • ~

I am reading a most interesting book about anti-gravity. I just can't put it down.

~ • ~

A cowboy was walking down the street with his new pet dachshund. The passer-by asked him why a cowboy would want to bought that kind of dog. The cowboy answer, "Well, somebody told me to get along little doggie."

~ • ~

A magician shows his agent a new act in which he makes 50 cigars appear out of thin air, takes a puff on each, and then swallows them one at a time until they're all gone.

"That's amazing," says the agent. "How do you do that with so many cigars?"

"Very simple," says the magician. "I get the cigars wholesale from a cousin in Tampa."

When his auto mechanic came in for a operation, Dr. Grimley couldn't help but take the opportunity to turn the tables on him.

"Well Frank," said the doctor, "It's going to take at least five days for the parts to get in. As for the cost, there's no way to tell until we get in there and see exactly what the problem is..."

~ • ~

For his wife's birthday party, a doctor ordered a cake with this inscription:

"You are not getting older,
 You are just getting better."

When asked how he wanted it arranged, he said, "Just put 'You are not getting older' at the top, and 'You are just getting better' at the bottom."

It wasn't until the good doctor was ready to serve the cake that he discovered it read:

"YOU ARE NOT GETTING OLDER AT THE TOP,
 YOU ARE JUST GETTING BETTER AT THE BOTTOM."

~ • ~

Our family has had many happy outings together. Trips to New York, Florida, all over the country. However, there was one December that will always remain our favorite. That was the time that we bought a wonderful camping tent on sale. We will never forget it...It was the winter of our discount tent.

Never get into an argument with the schizophrenic person and say, "Who do you think you are?"

~ • ~

Have you heard about the new teenage Barbie doll? As soon as you take her out of the box she starts to resent you.

~ • ~

A nun, a Priest, a Rabbi, an Irishman, a Scotsman and a blonde all walk into a bar. The bartender looks at them and says, "Is this some kind of joke?"

~ • ~

What do you call a hyperactive Irishman who keeps bouncing off walls?

Rick O'Shea.

~ • ~

Two atoms are walking down the street when they run into each other. The first says to the second, "Are you all right? You don't look so good."

"I'm not feeling very well," says the second atom. "I lost an electron!"

"Are you sure?" asks the first.

"Yeah, I'm positive!"

Two snakes were crawling along when one snake asked the other, "Are we poisonous snakes?"

The other replied, "You're darn right we're poisonous! We're rattlesnakes. Why do you ask?"

To which the first replied, "Because I just bit my tongue."

~ • ~

A man walks into a shoe store, and tries on a pair of shoes.

"How do they feel?" asks the sales clerk.

"Well ... they feel a bit tight," replies the man.

The assistant promptly bends down and has a look at the shoes and the man's feet.

"Try pulling the tongue out," offers the clerk.

"Nah, theyth sthill feelth a bith tighth." he says.

~ • ~

Just as a surgeon was finishing up an operation and was about to close, the patient awakes, sits up, and demands to know what is going on. "I'm about to close," the surgeon says.

The patient grabs his hand and says, "I'm not going to let you do that! I'll close my own incision!"

The doctor hands him the thread and says, "Suture self."

There's a famous fable concerning a skunk, a lion and a hawk who were debating as to which one was the most dangerous and feared animal in the jungle.

The hawk claimed top dog: "I win because I hit 'em from above, and from above, I have the best view of all. I can see things nobody else can!"

The lion rejoined: "Nonsense! I'm the most powerful animal of all, with the longest, sharpest teeth and claws. I'm the most dangerous, for sure!"

Then the skunk said: "I can stink up the whole jungle and run out every man or beast in the territory."

And so they argued, on and on, until a big old bear came along and swallowed the three of them, Hawk, Lion and Stinker!

~ • ~

Noah's remark as the animals were boarding the ark: "Now I've heard everything."

~ • ~

A man went to the Olympics and saw a young man walking around carrying a long, slender pole.

"Are you a pole vaulter?" he asked as the young man went by.

"Nein, I'm German. Und how did you know my name ist Valter?" he asked.

[This pun has all the worst elements of a joke because not only is it bad in its own right, but it requires an explanation - which makes it even worse. But I just can't resist anymore. So here, without further ado, is a painful excerpt from Isaac Asimov's own library of humor...]

"One of the basic equations of theoretical physics is e=hv, where v is the Greek letter nu (pronounced new). By simple algebraic manipulation, this is equivalent to v=e/h.

"Consequently, if one physicist were to ask another, "What's new?" it would not be surprising if the other were to answer, 'e/h?'"

~ • ~

All he asked for was a little good-night kiss, but she refused him with, "I don't do that sort of thing on my first date!"

"Well," he replied, "how about on your last date?"

~ • ~

A guy walks into a bar and notices two pieces of sirloin hanging from the ceiling. He asks the barman about it and the barman replies, "It's a competition. If you can jump high enough to get the meat down you get dinner on the house. But if you miss you have to buy a round for the whole bar."

The guy thinks about it and says, "No, I don't think so... the steaks are too high!"

The summer band class was just getting underway when a large insect flew into the room. The sixth-graders, eager to play their shiny new instruments, tried to ignore the buzzing intruder, but eventually one student could stand it no more. He rolled up his music book and swatted the insect, then he stomped on it to ensure its fate.

"Is it a bee?" another student asked.

"Nope," he replied. " It's a bee flat."

~ • ~

One day the zoo keeper noticed that the orangutan was reading two books -- the Bible and Darwin's Origin of Species.

In surprise he asked the ape, "Why are you reading both those books?"

"Well," said the orangutan, "I just wanted to know if I was my brother's keeper or my keeper's brother."

~ • ~

I worked for a while at a Wal-Mart store, selling sporting goods. As an employee of Wal-Mart you are sometimes required to make store-wide pages, e.g., "I have a customer in hardware who needs assistance at the paint counter."

One night a tentative female voice came over the intercom system with the following message: "I have a customer by the balls in the toy department who needs assistance."

A guy walks into a talent agency with a dog, and says "I've got a great act...my dog can actually talk."

"Surrrre he can," replies the talent agent, "prove it."

So the fellow asks the dog, "What is on top of a building?"

"Roof, roof!" the dog replies.

"What does sandpaper feel like?"

"Rough, rough!" the dog replies.

The talent agent starts to get impatient as the man asks his dog, "Who was the greatest baseball player of all time?"

"Ruth, Ruth!" says the dog.

Finally the agent becomes fed up and kicks the pair out of his office. Once outside, the dog looks up at his master and says, "Should I have said DiMaggio?"

~ • ~

When the air traffic controllers went on strike in 1980, who was called in to take their place?

Why, Herve Villechaize (Tattoo from Fantasy Island) and Bob Barker, of course.

Tattoo would point to the sky and yell, "De plane! De plane!"

Bob Barker would yell, "Come on down!"

What's the difference between a Southern zoo and a Northern zoo?

A Southern zoo has a description of the animal on the front of the cage, along with a recipe.

~ • ~

Did you hear about the psychic midget who escaped from jail? The headlines in the newspaper read "SMALL MEDIUM AT LARGE."

~ • ~

A Spanish mother and a Jewish father name their daughter Carmen Cohen. The mother only ever calls her Carmen and the father only ever calls her Cohen. The result? She never knows if she's Carmen or Cohen.

~ • ~

How about the two old men, one a retired professor of psychology and the other a retired professor of history. Their wives had talked them into a two-week stay at a hotel in the Catskills. They were sitting around on the porch of the hotel watching the sun set.

The history professor said to the psychology professor, "Have you read Marx?"

To which the professor of psychology said, "Yes, I think it's the wicker chairs!"

Steven Spielberg was discussing his new project -- an action docudrama about famous composers starring top movie stars. Sylvester Stallone, Steven Seagal, Bruce Willis, and Arnold Schwarzenegger being courted for the top roles.

Spielberg hoped to have the box office "oomph" of these superstars, so he was prepared to allow them to select the composers they would portray.

"Well," started Stallone, "I've always admired Mozart. I would love to play him."

"Chopin has always been my favorite, and my image would improve if people saw me playing the piano," said Willis. "I'll play him."

"I've always been partial to Strauss and his waltzes," said Seagal. "I'd like to play him."

"Sounds great," said Spielberg. Then, looking at Schwarzenegger, he asked, "Who do you want to be, Arnold?"

Arnold replied, "I'll be Bach."

~ • ~

While visiting in Italy, Donavan met a sailor from Venice. Before long they found themselves in a tavern. After several hours of drinking the Italian finally slid under the table.

The Irishman staggered to his feet and announced... "I'm the first guy who ever drank a Venetian blind!"

Why didn't Noah do any fishing from the ark? Because he only had two worms.

~ • ~

Following is a supplementary bulletin from the Office of Fluctuation Control, Bureau of Edible Condiments, Soluble and Indigestible Fats and Glutinous Derivatives, Washington, D.C.: Correction of Directive 943456201, issued recently, concerning the fixed price of groundhog meat. In the above named directive, the quotation on groundhog meat should read, "ground hogmeat."

~ • ~

It was one week before finals at the University of California, Berkeley, and everyone in my comparative religion class was frantic because of all the complex words and ideas we needed to know. The professor had just finished reviewing an Eastern concept he identified as Taoist, when a frazzled student protested, "But you said that was a Buddhist belief!"

The professor looked up with a smirk and said, "I'm afraid not. You see, that was Zen. This is Tao."

~ • ~

"I'm so depressed, I had to put my dog down."

"Was he mad?"

"Well, he wasn't exactly pleased."

What did Mrs. Worm say to Mr. Worm when he came home late?

"What in earth kept you so long?"

~ • ~

Two birds are sitting on a perch. One says to the other, "Do you smell fish?"

~ • ~

Cowboy: "Well, I suppose you've been all right. You've been a decent horse, I guess. A bit slow sometimes, but a decent horse..."

Horse: "No, you idiot! I didn't ask you for FEEDBACK! I said I wanted my FEEDBAG!"

~ • ~

Radioactive cats have 18 half-lives.

~ • ~

One night a grasshopper hops into a bar, and the bartender turns to him and says, "Hi, little fellow, did you know that we serve a drink here that's named after you?"

The grasshopper looks at him with surprise and says, "You mean to say you have a drink named Irving?"

Two men were down on their luck and decided to paint houses to earn some extra money. To start their business they asked the pastor of a local church if he would be interested in their service. He agreed and the men went out to buy the paint. As they drove to the paint store they decided that they would mix half paint and half water to try to increase their profits.

When they finished the job they called the pastor outside to look at their work. "The color looks a little dull," the pastor said. "You boys didn't cut the paint with water did you?"

They hung their heads and confessed. The pastor was very firm with them and said, "You must repaint and thin no more."

~ • ~

Photons have mass!? I didn't even know they were Catholic...

~ • ~

What did the Zen Buddhist say to the hot dog vendor?

Make me one with everything!

~ • ~

Why is two times ten the same as two times eleven? Because two times ten is twenty and two times eleven is twenty, too.

~ • ~

I bought a rather unusual tree. It's twenty-four feet high and it cost a fortune. It's a bonsai sequoia.

A census taker approached a woman was sitting on a porch. After introducing himself, he said, "How many children do you have?"

The woman answered, "Four."

The census taker asked, "May I have their names, please?"

The woman replied, "Eenie, Meenie, Minie and George."

Confused, the census taker said, "May I ask why you named your fourth child 'George'?"

"Surely, because we didn't want any Moe."

~ • ~

[I'd like to say a personal thank you to Deborah for sending this gem in. By the by, if anybody's interested in brushing up on your Latin, Semper Fidelis means "Always Faithful."]

Hey Joe, just wanted to share this with you. The other day i was sitting with my mom (finishing up travel arrangements to go see my son graduate from marine corps boot camp) and was writing a letter to my son to let him in on the arrangements.

As I was finishing up the letter, my mom told me to put on the bottom (before my name) SUPERFLY. I said mom why do you want me to put superfly. She said thats what he always puts there. I said mom he's saying SEMPER FI (a marine corps salutation). Thanks for listening thought you might enjoy that. - Deborah B., Fox Lake, IL

Senators William Spong of Virginia and Hiram Fong of Hawaii sponsored a bill recommending the mass ringing of church bells to welcome the arrival in Hong Kong of the U.S. Table Tennis Team after its tour of Communist China.

The bill failed to pass, cheating the Senate out of passing the "Spong-Fong Hong Kong Ping Pong Ding Dong Bell Bill."

~ • ~

"They have a Dial-a-Prayer for atheists now. You can call up and it rings and rings but nobody answers." - Tommy Blaze

~ • ~

"Everything is drive through. In California they even have a burial service called Jump-in-the-Box." - Will Rogers

~ • ~

A one-dollar bill met a twenty-dollar bill in the cash register of a local grocery store. "Hey, where have you been? I haven't seen you around here much."

The twenty answered, "I've been hanging out at the casinos, went on a cruise and did the rounds of the ship. I just got back to the United States recently, went to a couple of baseball games, to the mall, that kind of stuff. How about you?"

The one dollar bill said, "You know, same old stuff - church, church, church."

What did the mushroom say when he was kicked out of the nightclub?

"Don't kick me out, I'm a fun-guy!"

~ • ~

They're a perfect match. She's a real estate broker and he has a lot to offer.

~ • ~

What do you call a fish that can communicate in Binary?
A data bass.

~ • ~

A happily married man had only one complaint, his wife was always nursing sick birds.

One November evening, he came home to find a raven with a splint on its beak sitting in his favorite chair. On the dining room table there was a feverish eagle pecking at an aspirin while in the kitchen his wife was comforting a shivering little wren that she found in the snow.

The furious spouse strode over to where his wife was toweling down the cold little bird. "I can't take it any more! We've got to get rid of all of these darn..."

The wife held up her hand to cut him off in mid-curse. "Please Dear," she said, "Not in front of the chilled wren."